THE BUSINESS OF WAR

Recollections of a Civil War Quartermaster

WILLIAM G. LE DUC

Foreword by Adam E. Scher

DISCARD

MINNESOTA HISTORICAL SOCIETY PRESS

www.mnhs.org/mhspress

The Minnesota Historical Society Press
is a member of the Association of American University Presses.

Manufactured in the United States of America

10 9 8 7 6 5 4 3 2 1

⊗ The paper used in this publication meets the minimum requirements of the American National Standard for Information Sciences—Permanence for Printed Library Materials, ANSI Z39.48-1992.

Cover: Yorktown, Virginia, May 1862, Library of Congress, LC-B8184-B82
Pictures on pages iv and vi: Minnesota Historical Society collections

International Standard Book Number 0-87351-508-0 (paper)

Library of Congress Cataloging-in-Publication Data

Le Duc, William Gates, 1823–1917.
This business of war : the recollections of a Civil War quartermaster /
William G. Le Duc ; foreword by Adam E. Scher.
       p.   cm.
   Originally published: St. Paul, Minn. : North Central Pub. Co., c1963.
With new foreword.
Includes bibliographical references.
ISBN 0-87351-508-0 (pbk. : alk. paper)
   1. Le Duc, William Gates, 1823–1917.
   2. United States—History—Civil War, 1861–1865—Personal narratives.
   3. United States—History—Civil War, 1861–1865—Logistics.
   4. Soldiers—Minnesota—Biography.
   I. Scher, Adam, 1960–
   II. Title.
E601.L4 2004
973.7'8—dc22   2004008636

This Business of War

To my children and grandchildren
These recollections of my life are written
For their information and instruction

WILLIAM G. LE DUC

Foreword

ADAM E. SCHER

IN THE AFTERMATH of a crushing defeat at the Battle of Chicka-mauga in September 1863, the Union Army of the Cumberland un-der the command of Major General William Rosecrans retreated to the city of Chattanooga, Tennessee. Rosecrans ordered his troops to prepare defensive positions around the city and wired Washington to send reinforcements to prepare for the attack he knew was coming. The Confederate Army of the Tennessee, commanded by General Braxton Bragg, had wisely chosen to seize the nearby heights of Mis-sionary Ridge, Lookout Mountain, and Raccoon Mountain, effectively surrounding the Union forces. With their river and railroad supply routes severed, the Federal army was forced to employ a brutal sixty-mile wagon road through mountainous terrain to transport provi-sions. Bragg was intent on starving Rosecrans's army into submission and was achieving great success. Food was in such short supply that Union soldiers began pilfering feed from their horses and mules.[1]

To alleviate the suffering, a quartermaster from Hastings, Min-nesota, named William Le Duc was ordered to build a flat-bottomed steamboat and ferry rations to the army.[2] The craft was hastily con-structed and rushed into service before the upper works were fin-ished, the smokestack being installed en route. On a stormy night in October 1863, Le Duc and the crew of the USS *Chattanooga* set out on the Tennessee River from their base at Bridgeport, Alabama. In tow were two barges bearing 40,000 rations destined for the starving Fed-eral garrison, which included some of Le Duc's friends and neighbors in the Second Minnesota Regiment.

As the *Chattanooga* made her way downriver, the crew spotted a campfire on the shore. "Halloo! there. What troops are those!" called

The USS Chattanooga *on the Tennessee River, October 1863*

out a crewman from the steamer. "Ninth Tennessee," a sentry replied in a southern drawl, "Run your old tea kittle ashore here, and give us some hot whisky." Wishing not to have such a valuable cargo fall into enemy hands, the crew maneuvered the boat toward the opposite bank. "Who's in command?" cried Le Duc to a shadowy figure onshore.

"Old Stokes, you bet," was the reply. The *Chattanooga* had reached the Union outpost near Kelley's Ford commanded by Colonel William Stokes. News of the tug's arrival brought elation to the besieged Federal troops. "The soldiers were jubilant," recalled Le Duc, "and cheering 'The Cracker Line is open. Full Rations, boys! Three cheers for the Cracker Line,' as if we had won another victory; and we had."[3]

Once resupplied, Union forces waged a triumphant assault on Missionary Ridge in November, sending Bragg's troops in retreat southward toward Dalton, Georgia. Opening the "Cracker Line" saved the Army of the Cumberland and earned William Le Duc the enduring gratitude of his fellow soldiers. It was his greatest achievement as a Civil War quartermaster, due in no small measure to an indomitable spirit cultivated by an enterprising civilian life.

William Gates Le Duc was born on March 29, 1823, in Wilkesville, Ohio, into a family that made a modest living as farmers, but the young man had little interest in agriculture. "Life on the farm was not attractive to my parents or any of their children," he remembered. Determined to make a better life for himself through education, he enrolled at Kenyon College in Gambier, Ohio, where he studied Greek oration. Upon graduation in 1847, he began law studies with a firm in nearby Mt. Vernon, Ohio, the hometown of his fiancée, Mary Elizabeth Bronson. William was intent on moving to Booneville, Missouri, to practice law when he contracted cholera in 1850. Le Duc's cousin advised him to seek a destination farther north to avoid further contact with the disease, which had reached near epidemic proportions in the St. Louis area. William longed to be on the frontier, so his relative suggested heading up the Mississippi River to the new territory of Minnesota. Le Duc was intrigued and shortly after his recovery headed to Chicago, then across Illinois to Galena where he boarded the steamboat *Ben Franklin* bound for St. Paul.[4]

Le Duc arrived in Minnesota on July 5, 1850, and found St. Paul "a straggling frontier town, scattered over a narrow bench of land, ninety feet or so above the river."[5] The city was bustling thanks to a thriving fur trade with Canada and two river landings that provided berths for steamboats to inundate the town with goods on a daily basis. Settlers from across the nation and the world were arriving by the thousands, making St. Paul a melting pot of cultures and characters as witnessed by Pennsylvanian William McFarlane:

> I have been in some few towns in my journey through life but a more motley crowd than stood on the landing at St Paul I have never saw in any town of its size. Irishmen, Dutch, Californians, nigers [*sic*], omnibus drivers, Boatmen, speculators, Dandys, Gamblers, Winnebagos & Sioux Indians, half breeds, Frenchmen & Hosts of others too numerous to mention.[6]

St. Paul's early growth was largely the result of its proximity to Fort Snelling, located several miles upriver at the confluence of the St. Peter (later renamed the Minnesota) and Mississippi Rivers. A boisterous fur trader named Pierre Parrant, known as "Pig's Eye" because of a peculiar facial feature, had built a successful business selling whiskey to squatters residing near the fort. But an overindulgence in alcohol combined with a growing number of refugees near the garrison compelled army commanders forcibly to relocate the squatters downriver, and by 1840, nine cabins lined the riverbank of what would become downtown St. Paul. Parrant moved his saloon to a shack at the foot of present-day Robert Street, and because of his distinctive appearance and his popular establishment, river travelers began referring to the frontier town as Pig's Eye. But the settlement was destined to take a different name in 1841 when a Catholic priest named Lucian Galtier built a log church in town and dedicated it to St. Paul.[7]

Soon after his arrival, Le Duc established a modest but comfortable home at Third and Wabasha Streets. He then returned to Ohio where he and Mary Elizabeth Bronson were married on March 25, 1851. The Minnesota frontier to which he brought his bride was a significant transition for her. In contrast to William's agrarian upbringing, Mary's was one of sophistication. Her father, the Reverend Anthony Bronson, was a church rector who had also studied medicine. During her youth Mary traveled with her father to Boston and New York City where she became acquainted with the pursuits of a gentle nature. William wrote that Minnesota was "a great remove from her mother's handsome house in Mt. Vernon, Ohio, where . . . she was surrounded by comfort and all the elegancies of civilized life usual in a little city in the interior of Ohio, which she gave up cheerfully to begin here the founding of a home of her own." Their first years in Minnesota were imbued with an optimistic spirit shared by many couples in the frontier town. "Other young people in St. Paul were not better off than we were," recalled William, "and all were hopeful, young and happy, content with the life before us."[8]

Le Duc's satisfaction with his new surroundings failed to temper his entrepreneurial aspirations. He was soon engaged in various commercial ventures, establishing a law office on the corner of Third and Robert Streets and opening a book and stationery store across the street. Le Duc's affinity for travel also created opportunities to expand his business and civic associations. He mapped portions of the St. Peter River during a steamboat expedition; drew up a charter for the Lake Superior and Mississippi Railroad, which was the first railroad chartered in Minnesota; represented Minnesota at the World's Fair at New York City's Crystal Palace in 1853; and reported on the 1851 treaty at Traverse des Sioux, where Dakota Indians ceded their land to the United States.[9] Le Duc also cultivated strong friendships with influential figures like Henry H. Sibley, Henry M. Rice, and Ignatius Donnelly, each of whom later held state and national political offices.

In 1854 Le Duc further expanded his business holdings when he purchased a one-quarter interest in the townsite of Hastings, Minnesota.[10] Situated approximately thirty miles southeast of St. Paul at the confluence of the Mississippi, St. Croix, and Vermillion Rivers, Hastings was a thriving young community. William saw great potential in the river town and invested additional resources in its development. He organized the Hastings Ferry Company, developed a prosperous flour mill on the Vermillion River, and chartered the Hastings and Dakota Railroad Company.[11] Having successfully invested in Hastings, Le Duc closed his stationery store in St. Paul and moved his family into a house adjacent to his flour mill at Vermillion River Falls. In the years just prior to the Civil War, Le Duc remained occupied with business enterprises, including two farms on the outskirts of Hastings, and travels to Mary's hometown of Mt. Vernon, Ohio. William also began plans for the construction of a new home in Hastings that would serve as the family residence for more than half a century.

In 1861 the country erupted into civil war, and Minnesotans united in a wave of patriotism that swept through the North following the Confederate attack on Fort Sumter. Although a state for just three years, Minnesota was eager to participate in the national conflict. Governor Alexander Ramsey quickly offered a thousand men, making Minnesota the first state to volunteer troops for the Union army. Those who answered Lincoln's call came from all walks of life — farmers, clerks, attorneys, and teachers — and ranged in age from teenagers to men in their forties. Some joined out of patriotism or a hatred of the rebels. Many saw the conflict as a chance for adventure and travel. What they ultimately shared was a sense of duty that would be strengthened by the hardships of war. Nearly twenty-two thousand Minnesotans served in the conflict, with the state fielding eleven infantry and two cavalry regiments, an independent infantry battalion, two independent cavalry battalions, a heavy artillery regiment, three light artillery batteries, and two companies of sharpshooters. Most of these units would serve in the West against Confederate armies in Kentucky, Tennessee, Arkansas, Mississippi, and Alabama.[12]

Following the outbreak of hostilities in 1861, William Le Duc sought the counsel of a friend in the military and asked how he could best serve the country. The West Point graduate and Mexican War veteran suggested that William's experience in commerce would make him well suited for the Quartermaster Department, which held responsibility for supplying the troops. "This is a very important department of army service," Le Duc's comrade remarked, "No army can be efficient without the prompt exercise of their duties."[13]

In fact, the Quartermaster Department had a distinguished history of serving the needs of the combat soldier since the American Revolution. Established by the Second Continental Congress in 1775, the army's first quartermaster general, Major General Thomas Mifflin, operated the department virtually without resources and called upon many of the nation's newly formed states for supplies. Shortages incurred at Valley Forge encouraged the creation of a depot system for supply storage and distribution, which was established by the third quartermaster general, Major General Nathaniel Greene. Improvements in the management and transportation of army property were the hallmarks of Brigadier General Thomas Sidney Jesup, who served as quartermaster general from 1818 to 1860.[14]

When Jesup died in office on June 10, 1860, President James Buchanan needed to find a successor to fill the post. Secretary of War John B. Floyd successfully promoted the selection of a fifty-three-year-old cavalry officer named Joseph E. Johnston. An experienced artillerist and engineer, Lieutenant Colonel Johnston had been brevetted in both the Seminole and Mexican Wars. He was appointed quartermaster general and commissioned a brigadier general on June 28, 1860. Although expectations for his performance were high, Johnston's stamp on the department was minimal, for his tenure lasted only ten months. A native of Virginia, Johnston reluctantly tendered his resignation on April 22, 1861, three days after learning that his state had voted to secede from the Union. Ironically, prior to his resignation, Johnston approved the orders to equip the first 75,000 Union volunteers called to service by Lincoln. In succeeding years, Johnston became one of the South's most effective generals, commanding armies in Virginia, Tennessee, Georgia, and Mississippi. Nearly one-fourth of the Quartermaster Department's staff resigned to join the ranks of the Confederacy, including the future Confederate quartermaster general, Captain Abraham C. Myers of South Carolina. With the country mobilizing for war, President Lincoln quickly filled Johnston's vacancy by appointing Major Ebenezer S. Sibley, a twenty-three-year veteran of the Quartermaster Department, as acting quartermaster general.[15] A Herculean task lay ahead for the next quartermaster general, and Lincoln understood the significance of making a judicious appointment to the post.

When William Le Duc entered the service on May 8, 1862, the Quartermaster Department was in the capable hands of Brevet Brigadier General Montgomery Cunningham Meigs. Born in Augusta, Georgia, in 1816, Meigs was the son of Dr. Charles Dulcena Meigs and

Mary Montgomery Meigs. A descendent of Revolutionary War officers, Meigs quit the University of Pennsylvania to enter the United States Military Academy in 1832. Graduating fifth in his class in 1836, Meigs had the opportunity to enter any branch of service he desired. He began his tour of duty with the First Field Artillery but transferred to the Corps of Engineers, where he remained until his appointment as quartermaster general in 1861. Captain Meigs had distinguished himself before the war as the designer and builder of Washington's aqueduct and as construction superintendent for the U.S. Capitol wings and dome. In May 1861 Meigs was promoted to full colonel for his role in a clandestine mission to relieve the garrison of Fort Pickens at Pensacola, Florida.[16]

Twenty-four hours later he was nominated as quartermaster general with the rank of brevet brigadier general. Secretary of War Simon Cameron objected to the appointment of Meigs because of his role in the Fort Pickens expedition. President Lincoln, however, found the engineer to possess "the qualities of masculine intellect, learning and experience of the right sort, and physical power of labor and endurance" to do the job.[17]

Fortunately, Meigs inherited a Quartermaster Department operated by an experienced staff. Nearly one-third of the officers had served in the department more than twenty years. But they faced the daunting responsibility of supplying a force many times the size of the prewar army of sixteen thousand without the benefit of reserve stocks of supplies. The absence of reserve equipment and clothing compelled the department to rely on state governments and the staff of individual regiments to supply troops in the early days of the war. Regrettably, many newly appointed regimental quartermasters were ignorant of government procurement procedures. Corrupt contractors took advantage of their inexperience, which resulted in procurement blunders and scandals.[18]

To facilitate the distribution of supplies throughout the country, the states and territories of the United States were organized into departments by geographic region. The quartermaster general would customarily appoint a chief quartermaster to each department, but during the war it was not unusual for a single officer to preside over two or three departments combined to form a division. The Military Division of the Mississippi under General Sherman in 1864, for example, was comprised of the Departments of the Ohio, Cumberland, Tennessee, and Arkansas. The chief quartermaster prepared supply and funding estimates, made payments for supplies, and filled requisitions for troops in his department. Ordinarily he would not operate on the front lines unless it was necessary to eliminate a supply delay.[19]

In the first few years of the war, depot quartermasters or quartermasters in the field purchased supplies under contract. In 1864 Congress reorganized the Quartermaster Department and centralized the procurement process, assigning purchasing responsibilities to division heads in the quartermaster general's office. Strict inspection guidelines and penalties for fraud were also enacted as part of the department's overhaul, which reduced the rampant waste and mismanagement of government funds that prevailed during the early years of the war. Under the department's reorganization, contracting procedures were legislated for the purchase of shoes, blankets, tents, knapsacks, haversacks, wagons, horses, mules, harness, forage, and construction equipment. These reforms were especially beneficial in the procurement of clothing, which often had a reputation for poor quality. In fact, the term "shoddy," which refers to fabric made from remanufactured materials, became a frequently used term to describe the condition of early war uniforms, overcoats, and blankets. *Harper's* correspondent Robert Tomes corroborated this circumstance, reporting that soldiers on the first day's march found their uniforms "scattering to the winds in rags, or dissolving into the primitive elements of dust under the pelting rain."[20]

Despite vast logistical challenges, the Quartermaster Department successfully supplied forces engaged on multiple fronts. Quartermaster General Meigs was proud of the fact that Union forces experienced shortages on only two occasions—during the Confederate siege of Chattanooga in 1863 and when the quartermaster fleet was unable to get supplies to General Sherman's army after the capture of Savannah in 1865. As a career soldier, Meigs was also pleased to have been in the field with the troops during these two instances of emergency.[21]

Although Meigs spent most of the war in Washington directing the operations of the department, he did find opportunities to visit the field. In 1864 he assumed command of General Grant's supply headquarters at Fredericksburg, and when Confederate General Jubal Early advanced toward Washington in July of that year, Meigs led a contingent of War Department employees into defensive positions around the city. The quartermaster general also personally supervised the resupply of General Sherman's forces at Savannah in 1865. On those occasions when Meigs was in the field, a cadre of experienced officers, many of whom had been groomed by the quartermaster general, continued to run the department with efficiency. These men were extremely dedicated to Meigs and to their mission, and the lack of promotions bestowed upon department staff was a source of frustration early in the war. Meigs took the matter to the secretary of war on multiple occasions, noting that many field officers with less distinguished careers were being promoted over those in the Quartermaster Department. It was only through the quartermaster general's persistence in this matter that greatly overdue promotions began to arrive in 1864.[22] By war's end, Lincoln's selection for quartermaster general had been proven astute. Under Meigs's able administration, the Quartermaster Department supplied an army of more than half a million soldiers, operated a large and sophisticated depot system, transported extraordinary amounts of men and matériel, and assumed responsibility for a national system of military cemeteries.

In 1862 Captain William Le Duc joined his Minnesota comrades in the Second Corps as assistant quartermaster to the Third Brigade commanded by Brigadier General Napoleon Jackson Tecumseh Dana.[23] A native of Maine, General Dana had recently been promoted after serving as colonel of the First Minnesota Volunteer Infantry Regiment. General Dana reported to Brigadier General John Sedgwick of the Second Division, who in turn reported to the Second Corps commander, Brigadier General Edwin V. "Bull" Sumner. Commanding the Army of the Potomac was Major General George B. McClellan, who was directed by President Lincoln to move forward from his position on the Virginia Peninsula toward the Confederate capitol of Richmond. By proceeding up the Peninsula, McClellan hoped to avoid suffering high casualties caused by a march south on Richmond from northern Virginia. McClellan's plan called for the Union navy to transport the army using the James and York Rivers to protect the army's flanks as it advanced on Richmond. McClellan began amassing troops and supplies at Fort Monroe in March 1862 and launched the campaign a month later. Union forces had laid siege to Yorktown and fought an indecisive battle at Williamsburg when Le Duc arrived at White House Landing on May 19. His first impressions captured the chaos of war and the impact it would have on his life:

> Steamers and sailing vessels of all sorts filled the stream, and crowded the landing. A large force of men were engaged in unloading stores, guns, ammunition, and every conceivable munition of war. We stepped from the deck of the steamer to the deck of Quartermaster

Wagner's wharf and storage barge; from the steady going ways of civil life into the very vortex of the cyclone of army life; and for three and a half years I was one of the atoms "in God's great storm that roared through the angry skies."[24]

Le Duc had to grasp quickly the organizational structure and operation of the Quartermaster Department in the field. As an assistant quartermaster of a brigade, Le Duc was responsible for two or more regiments, which ordinarily consisted of one thousand men per regiment. Each regiment was assigned a quartermaster-sergeant and a regimental quartermaster with the rank of lieutenant. The quartermaster-sergeant issued supplies to the troops and assisted the regimental quartermaster department with the management of supplies, including tents, equipment, wagons, animals, and harness. He also requisitioned supplies and received and issued clothing, forage, and supplies furnished by the regimental quartermaster department to the appropriate officers.

Two or more brigades formed a division, with two or more divisions making a corps. Division quartermasters held the rank of major and corps quartermasters the rank of lieutenant colonel. When several corps were formed to create an army, a chief quartermaster with the rank of colonel was assigned to disburse funds and supplies to his subordinates from a general depot. The chief quartermaster of the army also received monthly reports from his department on the condition of property and the quantities that were required. In the early years of the war, these estimates went to Quartermaster General Meigs in Washington. By 1863 Meigs had assigned supervisory quartermasters to this task in order to simplify the disbursement process. Major Robert Allen, stationed in St. Louis, supervised activities for the Departments of the Northwest, Missouri, Tennessee, and Kansas. Colonel Thomas Swords, stationed at Louisville and Cincinnati, managed operations for the Departments of the Ohio and Cumberland. The Washington Depot commanded by Major Daniel Rucker supplied armies operating in the East.[25]

One of Le Duc's essential tasks was the requisitioning of supplies from depots for distribution to the troops. Small depots, located immediately to the rear of a combat zone, supplied soldiers with their daily needs, including rations, ammunition, and forage. The depot at White House Landing where Le Duc reported to assume his duties as assistant quartermaster was such an example. Larger general depots were situated in major cities with transportation networks that could distribute supplies to departments in designated geographical areas. New York, St. Louis, Fort Leavenworth, and San Francisco operated general depots and handled impressive quantities of goods during the war. The St. Louis general depot, for instance, purchased 8,864,173 bushels of corn, 377,518 tons of hay, 6,638 wagons, 100,364 horses, and 75,329 mules under the supervision of Major Allen. On those occasions when advancing armies found their supply lines stretched too thinly, quartermasters would establish temporary or advance depots. The Nashville Depot served as an advance depot to supply General Sherman's army in the Atlanta campaign. In the East, the depot located on the James River at City Point, Virginia, functioned similarly for General Grant during the Petersburg-Richmond campaigns of 1864–65.[26]

In June 1862 the depot at White House Landing from which Le Duc had been drawing supplies was evacuated as Confederate forces poured down from northern Virginia. After engaging General Joe Johnston's army south of the Chickahominy River near the towns of Seven Pines and Fair Oaks, the Army of the Potomac established a new base of operation at Harrison's Landing on the James River. Le Duc was assigned the task of planking a rail bridge over the Chickahominy as part of the withdrawal, and the rain-swollen river made the process of moving wagon trains especially treacherous.[27]

Army wagon trains generally consisted of headquarters, regimental, and supply trains. Supply trains carried rations, clothing, and other goods from base depots to temporary, smaller depots in the field. Headquarters and regimental trains primarily transported baggage and other supplies, including hospital stores. In optimal conditions, an army wagon with four horses could carry 2,800 pounds, and a six-mule team could carry 3,730 pounds, plus 270 pounds of forage. But conditions for the Chickahominy crossing were far from ideal. "The roads are execrable," Le Duc wrote in his diary, "and even on the high ground and knolls, the wheels cut through frequently to the axles."[28]

Once the Third Brigade was established at its new camp across the river, Le Duc set about improving the mess for General Dana and his officers. From Washington he secured tables, pots and kettles, flatware, and rations that included "a supply of canned goods, dried fruit, and several cases of sardines in oil." He also managed to purchase a supply of sweet potatoes from a local farmer for three dollars a bushel. Supplying rations to the troops was handled not by the quartermaster, but by the army's Subsistence Department, which purchased supplies in bulk from markets in Boston, New York, Philadelphia, Baltimore, Washington, Cincinnati, St. Louis, Louisville, and Chicago. After carrying out its inspection and packing duties, the Quartermaster Department transported the rations to field depots. Flour and beef were excluded from this process, both being procured in proximity to the armies. The prescribed army ration was bland and, by contemporary standards, not very nutritious. In camp, a Union army soldier was to be issued salt pork or bacon, bread or cornmeal, beans, rice, desiccated vegetables, coffee, sugar, vinegar, molasses, and salt. Potatoes, hominy, peas, onions, or canned tomatoes could also be served if practicable. Whiskey was provided only in case of "excessive fatigue and exposure." On the march, soldiers had to be content with salt pork, sugar, coffee, salt, and the dreaded hardtack, a flour-and-water cracker that often had to be softened in coffee or stew to be rendered edible. Small quantities of potatoes, onions, dried fruit, pickles, and sauerkraut were occasionally issued in the field to prevent scurvy.[29]

To lessen the monotony of army fare, soldiers would rely on packages from home or purchase delicacies from traveling merchants called sutlers. Occasionally the quartermaster would exploit an opportunity to embellish the soldiers' diets, as when Le Duc purchased a schooner-load of oysters from a boatman on the Potomac River.

For his efforts in planking the rail bridge over the Chickahominy and clearing the White Oak Swamp road, Le Duc was promoted to the rank of lieutenant colonel and assigned as chief quartermaster of the Eleventh Corps in November 1862. In 1863 the Eleventh was engaged at Chancellorsville and Gettysburg before being dispatched to Tennessee along with the Twelfth Corps to aid the Army of the Cumberland at Chattanooga. Prior to their departure, Le Duc was ordered to turn in his experienced mule teams and acquire fresh animals in Nashville. "The corral there was supplied with broken down and young, unbroken mules—colts," he recalled.[30]

Le Duc's dissatisfaction with the selection of animals was a prevalent complaint among army quartermasters. By taking advantage of a lack of a centralized procurement system, unscrupulous contractors and middlemen defrauded the government of vast sums by selling animals of inferior quality. By 1864 however, quartermaster officers were assigned to oversee the acquisition, inspection, subsistence, and transportation of horses and mules.[31]

Le Duc later shipped his seasoned mules from Virginia to replace the teams he was issued in Nashville. In addition to the task of finding good draft teams, Le Duc and his quartermasters faced the logistical challenge of transporting troops, equipment, rations, munitions, and other supplies from Virginia to Tennessee. This was largely accomplished by railroads, which were under the civilian control of the Office of the Director and General Manager of Military Railroads, with the Quartermaster Department serving as procuring agent. Although commanding generals in the West managed military railroads early in the war, by 1864 a uniform standard of civilian operation and maintenance was implemented for all theaters of operation. The Quartermaster Department was also responsible for ocean and inland waterway transportation. The department chartered more than seven hundred ocean steamers and built more than two hundred ocean-going vessels during the war. To facilitate maritime travel through hostile waters, the Quartermaster Department constructed and equipped a fleet of river ironclads that was ultimately transferred to the navy.[32]

In November 1863 Le Duc was detached from the Eleventh Corps and assigned to construct a supply depot at Bridgeport, Alabama. Although this was an important assignment, Le Duc was disappointed to learn that being severed from the corps brought a reduction in rank and pay. Nevertheless, he set about preparing for the task by sending for several civilian employees from his business operations in Minnesota. Le Duc oversaw a detail of more than three hundred men that transformed the post into a hive of activity. In addition to transporting substantial quantities of supplies to soldiers in the field on a daily basis, Le Duc's men built and equipped two steamboats, a boat landing, two warehouses, four repair shops, and four sawmills, which operated at a capacity of forty thousand feet of planking per day.[33]

His days were long, as chronicled in a letter to his wife on November 20:

> I am out soon after daylight, write up what letters and dispatches have come, get breakfast, mount a horse, and am not much in my tent until night. First I go to the steamboat landing to see if they are pushing forward the stores; next to the railroad station, to see what goods have arrived, and if the teams are loaded promptly, and sent to their destination. Next to the sawmills, to note the lumber on hand; next to the ship yard, to note progress on the steamboat, and hurry the work if possible; then to look after the coal-pit, and the new buildings; then, perhaps, to the other side of the river to look after a train of cars I have made up on that side. . . . Having gone through all this once or oftener, and having arranged the business of tomorrow, then I have

supper, and reports—letters and such—until ten or eleven o'clock, or later, as the exigencies of work may require. Then I snatch a few hours sleep, and begin it all over again in the morning.[34]

Reassigned to the Twentieth Corps and re-instated as a lieutenant colonel in April 1864, Le Duc participated in the Atlanta campaign and weathered conflict with its architect, General William T. Sherman. Le Duc and Sherman were former classmates at the Howes' Academy in Lancaster, Ohio, and had become reacquainted during the course of their service in Tennessee. Their relationship was convivial, and Le Duc praised "Cump" Sherman's professional abilities, hailing the general as one of the greatest military minds of the war. But Le Duc may have developed misgivings when Sherman appointed an acquaintance from Fort Leavenworth to be his chief quartermaster. As a military post quartermaster, Sherman's new supply officer was unfamiliar with field operations and had, in Le Duc's opinion, grossly underestimated the needs of the army on campaign.[35]

As a precaution, Le Duc assembled nearly seventy additional supply wagons and three hundred mules for his corps, concealing them along the route. His decision proved to be a shrewd one, for those who had followed the explicit orders of Sherman's chief quartermaster were forced to send back to Chattanooga for more supplies. Le Duc became further disenchanted with Sherman when the general ordered him to oust the citizens of Atlanta from their homes and relocate them to a camp outside the city. He found the order distressing and believed that such a harsh act would tarnish Sherman's legacy. Le Duc conveyed his concerns to Sherman, but the general was undeterred. "I do not care a damn how others read it," Le Duc remembered Sherman replying, "I am making the history, and the citizens of this rebel town shan't eat the rations I need for my army."[36] Le Duc reluctantly complied with Sherman's command. Despite their differences, the men remained cordial and even exchanged enthusiastic salutes at the Union army's Grand Review in Washington after the war.

Le Duc spent the remaining months of the war in Tennessee, witnessing the battle of Franklin in November 1864, and then in Washington where he served on a quartermasters examination committee. On March 13, 1865, he was brevetted a brigadier general for "efficiency, intelligence, and zeal in the discharge of his duties" and was discharged from the army on August 1, 1865.[37]

Following a brief but much-deserved vacation with his family, Le Duc returned to Hastings to begin the next chapter of his life with his wife, Mary, and their three children, Mary Elizabeth, Florence Gray, and William Bronson; their fourth and last child, Alice Sumner, arrived in 1868. Le Duc entered into a series of unsuccessful railroading and mining ventures that plunged the family into debt and left him somewhat disillusioned about the future. He returned to the family business of agriculture and recouped enough money to restore a portion of his wealth. Although Le Duc never possessed a strong affection for farming, he was interested in agricultural issues. He lectured at Grange Society meetings, wrote an unpublished farmer's dictionary, and corresponded extensively with individuals engaged in agriculture.[38]

In 1877 Le Duc received an appointment to serve as commissioner of agriculture under President Rutherford B. Hayes. Arguing that a dependency on imported agricultural products was stifling America's potential for prosperity, he began investigating methods to encourage the domestic production of commodities like sugar and tea. Inspired by a sorghum sugar display at the Minnesota State Fair, he embarked on a nationwide campaign to promote interest in the plant. But Congress failed to support his funding proposal for research, and the sugar program faltered. Le Duc launched an equally aggressive drive to put forward the domestic production of tea, which he estimated could save the nation up to twenty million dollars a year. In 1878 he engaged a planter named John Jackson to grow tea for the Agriculture Department on his Georgia plantation, but unsatisfactory results coupled with tepid support from Congress compelled Jackson to abandon the farm in 1880. A year later, however, Congress funded a grant for a tea farm in Summerville, South Carolina, and hired Jackson to manage the project. But the plantation required significant improvements that delayed the project, and by the time Le Duc left office in 1881, little had been accomplished.[39]

The Le Duc family savored the social, cultural, and educational opportunities of Washington and was bitterly disappointed when William failed to be reappointed to the commission. Returning to Hastings was especially difficult for Mary Le Duc who on several occasions afterward attempted to sell the family home and move back to the nation's capital. William also missed the vitality of Washington but confessed to a former associate that, "I cannot afford to abandon my house here and must remain in this inclement winter climate and debarred from society of many friends whom I would meet there."[40] Despite misgivings about their choice of location, the Le Ducs maintained a small social enclave in Hastings and continued to interact with members of St. Paul society, including the families of railroad magnate James J. Hill and Governor Alexander Ramsey.

The Le Ducs also enjoyed passing time in their grand home on Vermillion Street. Patterned after the designs and ideas of landscape architect Andrew Jackson Downing, the Le Ducs' striking Gothic Revival villa provided a comfortable setting in which to raise a family. Completed in 1865 at a cost of nearly thirty thousand dollars, the estate was heralded by the *Hastings Independent* as "the nicest house in the state."[41] A stylish carriage house, ice house, and picturesque grounds complemented the handsome property. William took great pride in planning and maintaining the landscape, which included a flower garden, an apple orchard, and a wood grove for evening strolls. Mary assumed responsibility for the design and furnishing of the house. Using a floor plan from Downing's *Cottage Residences* as inspiration, Mary drew a reversed version and hired architect Augustus Knight to complete the plan. The final design used beige-colored limestone for the walls and incorporated a three-story tower and steep sloping roof. Although Mary had ambitious plans for furnishing the home, persistent cash-flow problems obliged her to decorate it with an assortment of simple family pieces. The library housed William's extensive collection of agricultural books, as well as children's books and nineteenth-century literature, and was a favorite room for reading and family socializing. During William's frequent travels, Mary managed the home and pursued genteel activities such as gardening, reading, writing poetry, and sewing. Daughters Florence and Alice took up their mother's interest in sewing and fashion and created Hastings Needlework, a cottage industry making tablecloths, napkins, mats, and other handmade goods.[42]

Despite advancing years, William maintained his appetite for travel and an active life. Business dealings in railroading and mining coupled with personal concerns brought trips to Mexico, California, North Carolina, and Washington state. He tended his orchards, studied agriculture, lectured, read, and fished. Le Duc also developed an interest in spiritualism and published a book on the subject shortly before his death.[43]

In 1904 his beloved Mary died, concluding a partnership that Le Duc described as "fifty-three years of unclouded happiness." Yet the pressing nature of financial obligations continued to cloud William's thoughts. By chance he received a one hundred thousand dollar bequest from the widow of former business associate and Civil War General Dan Butterfield, allowing him to repair the family estate and secure his children's future.[44] In 1917 Le Duc contracted pneumonia following a winter trip to Atlanta, and he died at his home in Hastings on October 30.

Following her father's death, Alice purchased a house in Minneapolis, and the remaining family moved there, retaining the Hastings home as a summer residence. In the 1930s, Le Duc family friend Carroll B. Simmons began to use the house for his antique business. The family sold the house and a portion of the surrounding property to Simmons in 1940, presumably to pay back taxes. In the 1950s, developers expressed interest in purchasing the house in order to build a shopping center on the site.

Wishing to see the Le Duc house preserved for future generations, Simmons donated the property to the Minnesota Historical Society in 1958, the first historic site to be acquired by the Society. Simmons continued to operate his antique business from the house until his retirement in 1986, when the Society assumed full responsibility for the property.[45] In 2004, following a series of renovations and upgrades to the house, the Society transferred ownership of the property to the city of Hastings, which contracted with the Dakota County Historical Society to operate the house as a museum.

Over the years, the Minnesota Historical Society also acquired, and continues to preserve, the Le Duc Family collection, including correspondence, financial records, diaries, scrapbooks, and artifacts.[46] Conscious of his role in Minnesota history, Le Duc annotated his writings for the benefit of posterity, and his children spent years carefully organizing the family papers in preparation for future research. Le Duc completed his autobiography in 1913 as an account for his children and grandchildren. One of the latter, Augustine Gardner, finally saw the book through to publication in 1963. It successfully incorporates selected portions of his letters and diaries to document his achievements as entrepreneur, Civil War quartermaster, and commissioner of agriculture.

The memoir perhaps is less effective in revealing a more complex life that was tinged with disappointment. Like many Civil War veterans, Le Duc endured a series of failed postwar enterprises and was plagued by chronic financial difficulties. Nevertheless he was widely respected for his honesty as a businessman and proficiency as a soldier and public servant. An active participant in developing the territory and preparing Minnesota for statehood, Le Duc also had the privilege to witness and take part in the opening of a frontier state, the fratricidal struggle of civil war, and the postwar rebuilding of the nation.

Notes

1. Silas S. Canfield, *History of the Twenty-First Regiment Ohio Volunteer Infantry in the War of the Rebellion* (Toledo: Vrooman, Anderson and Bateman, 1893), 160.
2. William G. Le Duc, "The Little Steamboat that Opened the 'Cracker Line,'" in Robert Underwood Johnson and Clarence Clough Buel, eds., *Battles and Leaders of the Civil War* (New York: Century Co., 1884, 1888), 3:676.
3. Ibid., 678.
4. William G. Le Duc, *This Business of War: Recollections of a Civil War Quartermaster* (St. Paul: North Central Pub. Co., 1963; St. Paul: Minnesota Historical Society Press, 2004), 22–23, 29–30.
5. Ibid., 31.
6. Letter from William K. McFarlane to Samuel W. Sharp, May 25, 1855, Curtis H. Pettit Papers, Minnesota Historical Society.
7. Ronald M. Hubbs, "Who was 'Pig's Eye' Parrant, Anyway?" *Ramsey County History*, 26 (Fall 1991): 17–18.
8. Le Duc, *This Business of War,* 34–37; Carole Zellie, *Final Report: The Le Duc-Simmons House: A Report on Research and Recommendations for Interpretation* (Prepared for the Minnesota Historical Society, Historic Sites Division, 1989), 115; Wayne Gannaway, "The Le Duc Historic Site: A House of Ideals," *Over The Years* (Dakota County Historical Society), 42 (Dec. 2001): 2.
9. Le Duc, *This Business of War,* 33, 36–38, 42.
10. Ibid., 63.
11. Zellie, *Le Duc-Simmons House,* 30.
12. Virginia Brainard Kunz, *Muskets to Missiles: A Military History of Minnesota* (St. Paul: Statehood Centennial Commission, 1958), 27, 69–70. See also Minnesota Board of Commissioners on Publication of History of Minnesota in the Civil and Indian Wars, *Minnesota in the Civil and Indian Wars, 1861–1865,* 2 vols. (St. Paul, 1890–93).
13. Le Duc, *This Business of War,* 66.
14. Erna Risch, *Quartermaster Support of the Army: A History of the Corps, 1775–1939* (Washington, D.C.: Quartermaster Historian's Office, Office of the Quartermaster General, 1962), 1–61, 181–217, 308–19.
15. Ibid., 333, 334, 339.
16. Russell F. Weigley, *Quartermaster General of the Union Army* (New York: Columbia University Press, 1959), 19, 23–24, 30, 62, 158–60.
17. Ibid., 162–65; Abraham Lincoln, *The Collected Works of Abraham Lincoln,* Ray P. Basler, ed. (Washington, D.C.: Lincoln Sesquicentennial Commission, 1959), 394–95.

18. Risch, *Quartermaster Support of the Army,* 335, 338–40.

19. Ibid., 389–90.

20. Ibid., 347; Robert Tomes, "The Fortunes of War," *Harper's New Monthly Magazine,* June 1864, p. 227–28.

21. Risch, *Quartermaster Support of the Army,* 452.

22. Weigley, *Quartermaster General of the Union Army,* 294–95, 298–301, 313–14; Risch, *Quartermaster Support of the Army,* 393–94.

23. Le Duc, *This Business of War,* 67.

24. Ibid., 67–68.

25. Risch, *Quartermaster Support of the Army,* 390–93, 430.

26. Risch, *Quartermaster Support of the Army,* 427, 431, 433; Major Robert Allen's Report, July 1, 1865, appended to Quartermaster General's Report, 1865, *Annual Reports of the Quartermaster General, 1861–1865,* 505–8, as cited in Risch, 429.

27. Le Duc, *This Business of War,* 74–76.

28. Risch, *Quartermaster Support of the Army,* 421, 423–24; Nathanial S. Dodge, *Hints on Army Transportation* (Albany, 1863), 7; Office of the Quartermaster General, Personal Narrative Reports, F.Y. 1864, II, 764 (Col. S. B. Holabird Report, February 21, 1867), Record Group No. 92, NARA; Le Duc, *This Business of War,* 76.

29. Le Duc, *This Business of War,* 78–79; Risch, *Quartermaster Support of the Army,* 384, 447–49.

30. Le Duc, *This Business of War,* 97–98, 100–101.

31. Risch, *Quartermaster Support of the Army,* 374–78.

32. Ibid., 397, 400–401, 404; House of Representatives, *Executive Documents,* No. 337, 40th Congress, 2nd Session, p. 4–113, 140–57; Risch, *Quartermaster Support of the Army,* 412.

33. Le Duc, *This Business of War,* 105–6, 112–13.

34. Ibid., 107–8.

35. Ibid., 114, 125, 123.

36. Ibid., 124, 128–29.

37. Ibid., 132–37; Colonel Fred Ainsworth, Chief, Record and Pension Office, War Department to Commissioner of Pensions, March 8, 1899, Record and Pension Office of the War Dept., Record Group 94.12, NARA.

38. Zellie, *Le Duc-Simmons House,* 35–36, 38–39; Gannaway, "Le Duc Historic Site," 3.

39. Ben F. Rogers, "William Gates Le Duc: Commissioner of Agriculture," *Minnesota History,* 34 (Autumn 1955): 288–91.

40. Zellie, *Le Duc-Simmons House,* 107–9; Gannaway, "Le Duc Historic Site," 14–15.

41. *Hastings Independent,* May 5, 1864.

42. Carole Zellie, *Historic Structures Report: The William Gates Le Duc House* (Prepared for the Minnesota Historical Society, Historic Sites Division, 1987), 9, 58, 80; Gannaway, "Le Duc Historic Site," 11, 12, 15–16; Zellie, *Le Duc-Simmons House,* 72, 99, 134–37.

43. Zellie, *Le Duc-Simmons House,* 66.

44. Le Duc, *This Business of War,* 35; Zellie, *Le Duc-Simmons House,* 43.

45. Zellie, *Le Duc-Simmons House,* 110–12; Gannaway, "Le Duc Historic Site," 16.

46. See William Gates Le Duc and Family Papers, 1760–1967, Minnesota Historical Society.

I

Family Matters

I regret that my parents have not transmitted to me a more extended knowledge of their forebears, for family records are important as well as interesting. But for the anxiety of my grandmother to keep her only child by her side there would have been preserved family papers and documents of great value and interest. My grandmother, Lucy Sumner, was the daughter of Lieutenant Colonel John Sumner of the Continental troops. He had been a captain in the French War — so called — and the short, straight blade, with single guard for the hand, now hanging in our hall, was the sword he wore in that expedition to Canada that wrested from the French the St. Lawrence and the Great Lakes, and secured to the English Hudson Bay Company the most valuable fur trade in the world.

The genealogy of Colonel Sumner may be found in a book entitled *The Sumner Family* (Samuel G. Drake, Publisher — 1854), in which it appears that the Sumners of Connecticut, New York, and also North Carolina, are descended from the Sumners of Massachusetts; and it is interesting to note the family characteristics as they appear in different and widely separated localities. From old Judge and Governor Increase — of Massachusetts — down to the last one of his kith or kin, a sturdy love of justice and obstinate defense of the rights of all men, at whatever risk or personal loss, has been a prominent trait.

Colonel John Sumner was actively devoted to the rebellion of the colonies against the English Government, and his training as a captain of Colonial Troops in the wars of the English and French in Canada fitted him for efficient service in the Continental Army.

He was a large, strongly built man, as most of the Sumners have been and are. He was quick to think and act, as was exemplified once in crossing the Connecticut River in the winter season, with his wife, in a sleigh behind a gentle but fast horse. He got on the river, and found the ice too thin for safety, and, getting down in front, to equalize the weight in the sleigh, he whipped the horse, urging it to its fastest speed, until, on the farther shore, his wife exclaiming: "Don't beat the horse — are you crazy?" He said: "Look back, Elizabeth, and see the track of water. Nothing but the speed of the horse saved us. He will never get another stroke of the whip — never. Thank God for his speed which brought us safely over!"

At the battle of Monmouth, in which he was reported as being in the thickest of the fight, he, with many others, on that frightfully hot day, was overcome, and never recovered from the effects of the sun. He died from a dropsy, there induced, February 7th, 1787. He was one of the officers who formed the Society of the Cincinnati, but, finding there was a feeling of jealousy among people who could not become members, he, with others of the Connecticut Chapter of that Society, relinquished his membership, as I found of record at the State House in Hartford.

On his deathbed Colonel John Sumner said to his wife: "I do not leave much for you and the children, but the money due for my services is unpaid, and they will pay you after a time, when prosperity comes — and it will come." But his heirs have never received a cent. The debt was acknowledged, but never paid.

He was married twice. By his first wife he had a son who was a surgeon in the U. S. Army, and afterward practised his profession in Wethersfield, and in Springfield, Massachusetts, where he died, leaving a daughter, Julia, who died without issue. Colonel Sumner's second wife was a Miss Reynolds, of Norwich, and the children of this marriage were seven — three boys, and four girls. One, Joseph, was master of a vessel, and died at sea. Another, Charles, died in the West Indies, of yellow fever. William — for whom I was named — emigrated to Ohio at an early day, and was Colonel of a regiment that marched to help General Harrison in the war of 1812. I have heard him narrate his march, and describe the camp he made in the thicket of brush that was where the city of Columbus, the capital of Ohio, now stands. He married the childless widow of Colonel Williamson, and left no children.

My grandmother was the only child of Colonel John Sumner who married and left heirs who gave promise of the continuation of this branch of the Sumner family. Lucy Sumner was married on the 23rd day of March, 1796, to Henri Duc, in Middletown, Connecticut, at her father's house, and the result of this union was one child, my father, Henry Savery Duc, or Le Duc, as he chose to write his name after arriving at middle age, because his aunt, Clarissa Sumner, told him his father had used the particle in France, and had omitted it here because he thought it more popular. I remember distinctly Aunt Clarissa's statement that it was a return to the original form of the family name.

Henri Duc was born in Lyons, France, November 25, 1762. He had been educated in one of the military schools of France, and was a young officer in the army sent from France to aid in the war of our revolution, and was, I think, with the French at the capture of Cornwallis. So far as known he was afterward with the troops left on the islands Guadaloupe and Martinique. He resigned, and became a sugar planter. At the time of the reign of terror in France, and the murder of the whites by the slaves in the Islands, he was hidden by his body servant in an empty sugar cask for fourteen days, and then got on board a Yankee trading vessel, and was landed, with his servant, in Middletown — where he married Lucy Sumner aforesaid.

He had a sister, Elizabeth, the eldest of his father's family, and a younger brother, Joseph, who lived with his sister, both parents being dead. The reason why so little is known of my grandfather's affairs is that soon after his death my grandmother burned all his papers and letters from abroad, and destroyed everything that would give information of his family in France, or his property in the West Indies. She said, in excuse, that her brother Charles had gone down to those hateful islands, and died of fever, and her brother Joseph had contracted there the disease of which he died on shipboard; and that she was the mother of an only child, and she would not have him seeking his father's property in the Islands, nor going to France to see his relatives. Whatever knowledge she possessed of his affairs or family perished with her.

Henri Duc, when he escaped from Guadaloupe, or Martinique, brought some money with him, and after a time went back and got more, with which he started a mercantile business in New York, in partnership with an Italian, who had charge in that city,

3

while my grandfather purchased cargoes of stuff coming from the Islands to the port of Middletown, from which sailed many trading vessels at that time. These cargoes he would personally conduct to New York.

On one occasion he found his Italian partner had departed for Italy, taking with him all the money he could raise, and leaving my trusting forebear to pay the debts. He assumed all obligations, and, taking a large house called the Woodbridge, opened it for a private hotel. He had acquired some interest with a Mr. Wilkes, in some land in Ohio, and, when his debts were all paid, he went out and made a settlement on a part of this land, calling it Wilkesville. Here he built a two-story brick house — the first in that part of Ohio — and here his wife and child joined him in A.D. 1811, and here he remained until his death, June 21st, 1827. He had secured a modest little competence, and was living happily, imitating, as far as possible, the ways of a chateau in his beloved France, with dependents about him, and a garden to which he loved to resort in the early morning and pick some flowers to ornament the table, or to place on his wife's pillow, when he would wake her with the admonition: "The sun is up, my Lucy — the birds are calling."

My grandmother told me she never knew of his exhibiting anger against any person, and never but once against anything — and the occasion then was one on which anger was justified. He had taken in hand a little lamb abandoned by its mother and perishing with hunger, and nursed it back to life, feeding it warm milk from a teaspoon. It had learned to know his voice and come at his call, and was much petted, and had the run of the front yard. Some careless person having left the gate open at night, a big black sow got into the yard, caught the lamb, and was eating it when he came out of the house and saw it. He ran to the gate, closed it, and, seizing a piece of wood, pursued the sow and beat it to death.

Some other traditions related to me of my grandfather are: When in the Woodbridge House he had as guests two young naval officers, Hull and McDonough, who afterward won great distinction. With these young officers he used to engage in sword exercise in which he was very skillful, a favorite diversion being to count the buttons on the vests of his opponents with the point of his rapier, in spite of their efforts to prevent. McDonough was restive and about to resign, and take employment in the merchant service, but yielded to my grandfather's remonstrance which saved him to the navy, and he afterward won his fame on Lake Champlain.

McDonough gave my father a one-keyed boxwood flute, which was, for several years, my treasured and sole musical instrument, and which is yet in my possession. It was while living in the Woodbridge House that my grandfather heard of the death of his idolized sister. Her miniature, a painting on ivory, he always carried on his person while he lived. This portrait, which descended to my sister Elizabeth, shows a beautiful, high bred woman of about 1790.

My grandfather was much respected and beloved. He was, indeed, as honest a man and as fine a gentleman as the state of Ohio ever had the honor of claiming as a citizen. My recollection of him is quite distinct. He was a man of medium size and pleasant face, who used frequently to take me on his knee and feed me soup from an ornamented china bowl, with a silver spoon that was some sizes too large for my mouth — much to his amusement. I was between four and five when he died. I remember his funeral, and the crowd of people that assembled, and my taking my next younger brother by the hand and leading him off after the procession, which I followed as best I could, dragging him up a long hill; and when the family returned from the funeral we were picked up and returned home.

The reign of terror had caused a company of French *émigrés* to come to America, and make a settlement they called Gallipolis on the Ohio River, near to Mr. Wilkes' tract of land. When my grandfather went out to Ohio he was accompanied by a friend of his early years, who, in France, had been a suitor for the hand of his sister Elizabeth, who had preferred and married some one else. His name was Savery, and my father was called for him — Henry Savery. My grandfather located Wilkesville about twenty-five miles north of Gallipolis, and Mrs. Savery, who was of a wealthy family in France, bought some of the Wilkes lands, and also lands nearer the Ohio River, and in Kentucky. He never married, and was a frequent visitor at our house until my grandfather's death.

The town of Wilkesville, as I remember it, was well located on comparatively level ground, with good drainage naturally, and was always a healthful place, and, for a country town not a county seat, was a center of considerable trade, and on the main traveled roads, from the Ohio River at Gallipolis to Chillicothe and Columbus and Lancaster — and also on the main road to Athens. It was laid out in rectangular form, streets running north and south, east and west. I remember but the two main streets and the public square, which cornered at the crossing of these streets, and lay to the northeast, while my grandfather's house was on a corner lot on the southwest; and my mother's brother, Willard Stowell, had a long, one-story frame building which he used as a store for general merchandise, and in which he did a very large business, buying up droves of horses, cattle, and hogs, to be driven to market across the mountains to Baltimore and Philadelphia.

My grandfather's house had a hall through the middle, and two rooms on each side, and stood back from the road, leaving a little front yard. A garden was in the rear, and then a field extending, according to my childish recollection, indefinitely, toward a creek and timber, and the fields extended southward along the street beyond my limited knowledge.

Life seemed to pass pleasantly and profitably after the cessation of the war with the British and their Indian allies. The frontier life had its enjoyments, as well as trials and self-denials. The incoming of new settlers, the selling of lands, the different little industries and shops established or promoted by my grandfather, and the visits of his countrymen to and from Gallipolis gave employment of mind and body, and, as his little village grew into a semblance of the surroundings of a chateau in France, he seemed to be content, but talked frequently of the property he had in the West Indies, and, but for the determined opposition of my grandmother, who's consent he could not obtain, he would have gone to New Orleans, and shipped from there to Martinique, or Guadaloupe, or wherever his possessions were. The memory of her two brothers lost in that region was such a terror to her that she thought certain death would be the consequence of a voyage to that fatal clime, and she urged that they could not be any happier if they had all the money in the Islands, and, as there were but themselves and one child, it was neither necessary or wise to take such a risk.

I was born March 29th, A.D. 1823, in Wilkesville, in the upper front room on the north side of my grandfather's brick house. My mother's name was Mary Stowell. She married my father when not yet seventeen years old, on the 15th day of April, A.D. 1820. The earliest recollection that I have is that of my baptism, which,

6

when I related it to my mother a few years before her death, she pronounced to be correct in every particular. I was taken from the house of my grandfather – one half of which my father and his family occupied – and, turning to the right we passed south down the street. I was a small child, just able to walk by reaching up and taking my mother's hand. After what seemed a long distance we turned to the left, across a rough bridge, going up a slight rise, and to the left was a double log cabin. In the room to the right were gathered some people with children to be baptised. The child who had a little water sprinkled on his face before me was alarmed and noisy. What I did I do not remember, but have been told that I was fighting mad, and kicked. I do recall the satisfaction I felt in getting out of the place and going home, wondering how people could wash faces in such a foolish, ineffectual manner.

A double log house, as made in Ohio in those early days, consisted of two pens of logs eight or ten feet apart, the space between the two pens – or houses – being covered by extending the roofs of each, and this interior space was generally left open on one side, and was used for storing saddles, bridles, harness, or anything that was likely to be carried off by wild animals – no protection against human thieves being necessary. And this served a good purpose until a new house could be built; then the double cabin would be converted into a stable or storehouse.

A few letters on some trivial matters in Ohio, and the miniature of his sister, are all that remain to us of my grandfather's effects. My grandmother effectually carried out her intention. I often questioned her when I was a boy, and also when arrived at man's estate, but either she had forgotten, or knew nothing definite, or did not wish to inform her grandchildren of anything that might take them to the West Indies, or to France. From my mother and Aunt Clarissa I obtained all I know of my grandfather, excepting the little I remember as a child. Aunt Clarissa told me that he was descended of a wealthy family, was educated for the army, and was a Catholic in his religion, as were almost all the people of France. But the day he left France, ordered on shipboard with the division of troops to which he was attached, he left the marching column to go a short distance and bid a lady farewell. Before her door he found the overshoes of the Bishop – which was notice that no one would be permitted to enter until he had come out – but, disregarding this notice, he went in, and the Bishop, indig-

nant at the intrusion, ordered him to depart, which he declined
to do until he had said good-bye to his friend. Then the Bishop
left in great anger, and his friend begged him to go quickly and
join the troops, as the Bishop would certainly send armed men
after him, and, if caught, he would never again be heard of outside prison walls. And he went, and was pursued by the Bishop's
men, until he found protection among the soldiers; and from that
time on he was a Catholic no longer.

Aunt Clarissa told me that, when he escaped to New England
from the Islands, his body servant, the Negro slave who came away
with him, had remained with him after his marriage until my
father had grown sufficiently to run around the house and yard;
and one unlucky day when grass was being pitched, the child got
in the way, and the prong of a fork struck his upper lip, cutting it
open, which so frightened the Negro that he ran away, and never
returned. She told me also that my grandfather had — beside
beautiful military and other clothing — a coat of silk woven
without a seam by the looms of Lyons.

II

Growing Up in Ohio

After the death and burial of my grandfather, my grandmother's brother, Colonel William Sumner, of Lancaster, Ohio, paid a visit, with his wife, to his sister at Wilkesville, and, as the result of a family conference, it was decided that I should go back with them to be sent to school, and to grow up in Lancaster. My uncle had what was known as a "dandy wagon" — a strong buggy of those days of rough roads, and no elliptic springs — in appearance very much like a covered, one-horse buggy of the present day. Into this I was easily pursuaded to enter, to take a ride, and left the place of my birth, never to see it again. We turned to the west, past my Uncle Willard's store, and after traveling an hour or more came to the farm of my grandfather — my mother's father. Here my trouble began. I insisted on stopping, but was not permitted. I had been taken out to this place at some previous time, riding on horseback behind one of my uncles, who discovered a large rattle-snake lying asleep across the road, and had quietly slipped off the horse, giving me the bridle to hold, while he got a branch of a tree, and killed the snake, and, pulling off the rattles, put them in my cap. I had remained at this farm for some weeks, until I had cut my thumb nearly off with a drawing knife, and had pulled the spigot out of a barrel of cider, to see how much of a stream I could make, when I was returned home in disgrace. Here I had once had a good time, and here I proposed to stay. My protests were clamorous, but vain, and on we went until we came to Raccoon Creek, then a stream requiring a ferryboat to pass over. Here, I thought, was the sea, or great water, over which I would not go, and I started my retreat on double quick, but my uncle or the ferryman

9

easily overtook and brought me back — kicking and yelling and fighting — and put me on the boat, and pushed off from shore. "Now," they said, "jump over, if you want to be drowned!" I did not like water well enough to wish to be drowned, and so remained, giving up further opposition to being carried away. The ferryman ferried us across. I felt now that I would never see my home again.

Our route was through the old Indian town of Chillicothe, where my uncle had friends, and we remained over night with Richard Douglas, then and afterward a noted wit and lawyer. He had two sons, Luke and Albert, teasing boys, older than I, who called me: "Cry-baby-cripsey," because I grieved to see my mother. I have never quite forgiven them. My next recollection is arrival at Lancaster, and introduction to the nieces of my uncle's wife, Hetty and Mary Herron, two grown girls, who, a night or two after our arrival, before I had the run of the house, and in the absence of the older people, when I asked them for a drink, told me to go to the sideboard, and pour some out of the bottle there. I poured out a full glass of whiskey, and, being thirsty, drank it down before it had time to burn, or they to object. I had never seen whiskey at my father's, and complained that the water was bad. When my uncle and aunt came home I was dead drunk, and they were anxious for fear it would close my earthly existence then and there.

The town of Lancaster was located upon the site of an old Indian village on the banks of the Hock-Hocking River, where it was crossed by the military road made by General Wayne, in his campaign against the Miamis and Wyandots in 1793-4-5, in the midst of one of the most fertile and healthful sections of Ohio — that paragon of states. As the Indians retreated the white settlers from Pennsylvania, Virginia, New York, and the New England states came in and opened farms in the dense forest, laid out a town, established mills, shops, tanneries, and brick yards. When I first saw the place it was the county seat of Fairfield County, with a court house, market house, churches, two respectable taverns, and a public school house — a two-story brick building, with an ample playground. I was placed in school here, in the room to the right, as we entered the hall, and my teacher was a Yankee named Parsons, and a faithful, excellent teacher he was. He was succeeded after a few years by a man named Roscoe, an expert bookkeeper, who remained in charge of the school I think only one year. He strongly insisted on our learning bookkeeping by the Italian system of double entry. I remember yet his foundation rhyme:

"By journal laws what you receive
Is debtor made to what you give," etc.

Two brothers, John and Mark Howe, purchased an old orchard, Boyle's, in the northern part of the town, and erected a large academy, or grammar school building, to which I was transferred, and where I remained under their tuition while in Lancaster. . . .

During my school days in the Howes' Academy the students were encouraged to give an exhibition in the third story, which was fitted up as a theater with curtains and stage accessories that were purchased from a defunct Thespian Society. We attempted the play called Pizzarro, written by an English authoress. I remember the difficulty someone had in adapting a cavalry jacket, man's size, to my boy's figure, and the tucks that were taken in the sleeves, and the pinnings and bastings necessary to make the little swallow-tails hang properly. The coat was blue, trimmed with yellow binding, with brass buttons in front, as worn by the cavalry soldiers of that day. "Cump" Sherman was Pizzarro. I was the soldier deputed to guard the Peruvian prisoner, Rollo. (Thus, it seems, I was General Sherman's first soldier; afterwards, under his command, I turned twelve thousand people out of their Atlanta homes.) In the play I had a short German gun, and as I marched out to take my place on the stage, with gun at "shoulder arms," the applause and shouting were noisy, but when the Indians approached me with bars of gold to buy the release of the captive, and I turned upon them with the indignant: "What — bribe *me* — an old Castilian?" and my little bob-tail coat was turned to the audience, the house went wild, and, my part being finished, I went off the stage without knowing until many years after, why I had so distinguished myself.

Among the recollections of my boyhood days is that of the Millerites' excitement concerning the end of the world. My uncle had a farm some few miles in the country, in charge of a farmer named Green, a poor white, who had emigrated from the mountains of Virginia — a man of good hard sense, though he could neither read nor write. He came to town with a load of produce,

11

and I had permission to go out to the farm and stay over night. Seated alongside the farmer, on — to me — a high seat, as we were going down a long hill, looking toward the west, the red sun, of large size, shown through the smoky haze of an autumnal atmosphere, and, getting up close to him, I said, in a frightened voice, "Mr. Green, do you know what they say down at the Baptist meetings?"

"No, boy; what do they say?"

"Why, they say that the world is coming to an end, and that the sun will get as red as blood, and be as big as a wagon wheel — and you just look at the sun!"

Green was an immense man, and, putting his hand on me, with a roar of contemptuous laughter, he answered: "Don't you be afeerd, little feller; there's bin sich damn fools always, an' I've heern jist sich fool things ever since I was a little feller like you, an' the world haint come to no end yit — and it aint goin' to as long as the good Lord has so much cawn ground to cl'ar up!" I have heard the same prediction many times since then, but have felt satisfied that the "cawn ground" was not yet all "cl'ared up."

I was fleet of foot when a boy, as I found one day when pursued by a racer snake, in my father's orchard. I went home with such speed as to discourage any reptile without wings. And another time, when living in Lancaster, I stood, with other lads, watching the firing of a cannon on the Fourth of July behind the man ramming the load, when a premature explosion occurred which blew off part of his arm, and I ran a quarter of a mile home — fear and horror lending wings to my feet — and reported the accident almost as soon as the sound of the discharge reached my uncle's house. I am sure I could go to the very place of the accident now.

My people in Lancaster attended the Presbyterian Church. The Reverend John Wright was pastor, and a man of learning, preaching according to the Presbyterian faith and methods of the time. I have no recollection of his preaching, but I was required to attend Church and Sunday School every Sunday. The Reverend Mr. Wright was old and feeble when he resigned his charge, and he went, with his wife, to Indiana, where his two sons had settled. He gave me, as something to remember him by, a book — a copy of the Koran — which I treasured for many years, though I always thought it a curious present from an old Presbyterian preacher to an immature boy. He was succeeded by the Reverend Mr. Cox, who became quite popular as a preacher and as a citizen of our town. . . .

My father, after the death of his father, closed up the estate, and moved to Amesville, a small town a few miles east of Athens, the county seat of Athens County. Here he opened a store of general merchandise, but finding the profits not large enough to support his large family, he closed out the business, and moved to a farm in Licking County, near Johnstown. This was two hundred acres of excellent land, entered by some scrip given to Colonel John Sumner, (my father's grandfather,) for services in the Revolutionary War. It was in the midst of the great forest then covering almost all the entire state of Ohio. About forty acres had been cleared and cultivated, an orchard of five acres of apple trees had been set out, and were in bearing condition; a double log cabin, built near a fine spring, and a log barn and stable comprised the improvements when first I saw the place, to which I was called from school in 1838 or '39. The country was rapidly filling up, farms being opened, a little village of traders and mechanics with doctors and an occasional preacher was growing, and my help was required on the farm.

A double log cabin was the shelter commonly built on the new farms opened in the Ohio woods. It served its purpose very well until sawmills and brick-yards were established, and nails and glass, with door trimmings, and other necessities for building were brought in by the traders. After the people had acquired money to buy these things, they erected better houses — that is, better in appearance, if not more comfortable. Log cabins were the only possible houses for the frontiersmen in the Ohio forest, and were very comfortable dwellings. Trees were selected of as nearly as possible the same diameter, (twelve to sixteen inches) with straight stems for the length desired, which was from twelve to sixteen or eighteen feet. The larger logs were placed at the bottom, and care was taken to choose good, sound oak or walnut logs for the sills. The logs were cut and dragged to the place selected by the team of the settler, (which was generally a yoke of cattle), and were distributed on the four sides of the proposed building. The settler having done all he could without assistance then invited his neighbors to a "raising bee", and they would willingly come from miles away to help the newcomer. Skilled axe men volunteered to take the corners, and cut, notch, and saddle. As the logs were put in place, they were "hacked and scutched" and dressed to a flat surface with a broad axe. When the pen had been carried to a height of about seven feet, joists (logs stripped of the bark,) were introduced to support an upper floor, if any boards could be obtained to make a floor. The sides were then carried up three feet, and the roof timbers put in place. These were straight logs, three feet apart, or according to the length of the shingles to be used. These shingles, or clapboards, as they were called, were rived out of straight grained timber (usually white oak), and were four feet long, about half an inch thick, and about seven or eight inches wide, and thinner on one side than the other, humoring the grain of the timber from which they were split.

The gable logs, first placed, were extended far enough to receive the butting, or drip log, for the first tier of shingles, which were laid on loosely — that is, without nailing, as there were as yet no nails to be obtained. This tier of shingles, or clapboards, as they were called, was held in place by another log running from gable to gable, and lying six or eight inches from the top of the first course of clapboards. In this way the cabin was roofed, and well protected from rain storms, but the snow would sometimes blow in through the clapboard roofs. The doors were hung on wooden hinges and secured by wooden latches on the inside, usually raised by a string attached to the latch, run through a gimlet hole above, and hanging on the outside. The floors were made of slabs split out of large or small trees, halved, and, in either case, the upper surface dressed with a broad axe or adze. The floors were replaced by board floors when sawmills were within reach. Boards were frequently carried by teams forty or fifty miles.

The tools desirable for use in building a log cabin were a chopping axe, a broad axe, two or three augurs of different sizes, cross cut saws, and handsaws, and an adze. A jackplane was desirable, but not absolutely necessary. A draw-shave and grindstone were also important adjuncts, and a meager set of carpenters' tools was a public benefit to the neighborhood.

I have been thus particular in describing the log cabin that you may know some of the trials of the frontier life in the forest of Ohio in the early part of the 19th century. After living a few years in the log cabin, it was possible to get lumber at a sawmill distant a day's travel. Thus it took two days to get a load of sawed stuff, and sometimes one had to wait a day while it was being sawed.

When my father commenced to build a frame house two stories in height, with a kitchen addition a story and a half, and a back porch, the lumber was first seasoned in the air. The hardwood flooring was dressed by hand, first planing it to a gauge of width. The recollection of the planing and grooving of that hardwood flooring makes my arm ache yet. But in time it was done, and a well dug at the end of the porch near the kitchen door, and the family moved from the good old log cabin into the new house. It was located near the main traveled road, and was a very comfortable farm house, with ample room for the family, and for a visitor or two. I had been brought home from school in time both for an experience in the log cabin, and to help build the new house.

Threshing was done with flails, and also with horses driven around the threshing floor, treading out the grain. I was much attracted by the flailing process, and admired the actions of the men in swinging the flails. Taking advantage of their absence, one day, I took up a flail, and tried to imitate their motions, with the result that I was hit on the head by the flying end of the flail, and laid out for a time. This satisfied me that I would not be a farmer. Previous to this I had earned my first money by dropping corn for a Mr. Kasson, for which I was paid eighteen cents a day. Kasson was a large, handsome, noble specimen of manhood, superior to most of the settlers around him, although he could neither read nor write. I admired him for his native politeness, and generous manliness. He liked me for the little book learning I possessed, and helped me to get a calf, which grew to be a fine steer. He was ready for the butcher, but on the morning I was to have sold him, he was found dead, and my expectations were dissipated.

I had determined to quit the farm, and somehow obtain a college education. A preacher, named Purinton, who had married my mother's sister, and was living in Warren, Trumbull County, Ohio, offered to help me prepare for the freshman class. I had six and a half dollars, and traveling on the Ohio canal was cheap. My father took me to Newark, and put me on a canal boat, and bade me Godspeed on my journey and quest.

In due time I arrived at Alton, where a branch canal connected with Warren. Stopping off here to change boats I was told that a freight boat had left only a short time before I arrived. Another person, — Agnew was his name — hearing my inquiry about the boats, said: "I too am going eastward, and I believe we can easily overtake the boat; I was employed in the engineer crew that surveyed this branch of the canal, and know it all." The result was that I joined the engineer in the pursuit of the boat, which, of course, could only go as fast as a team of horses or mules could draw it through the water. We started at a rapid walk on the tow path, and kept it up until sun down of that long summer day, before we overhauled the slow old freighter which had left Alton several hours before the time given us.

My companion, Agnew, being accustomed to marching, had led off at a quick gait that he kept up all the afternoon. I followed with difficulty. Finally, as the sun was about to set, and no boat in sight, I declined to go farther, and sat down on a log. Agnew said he would go to the bend where he could see a long tangent, and if the boat was in sight he would signal me, and go on and stop the boat until I could come up. This he did, and the boat was stopped until I crawled up, and was helped aboard. We had walked thirty miles that afternoon.

Arriving at my uncle's I gave a few months to Latin and Greek, and then finding an opportunity to teach a school a few miles east from Warren, in a farming neighborhood, I engaged for three winter months. I do not remember the compensation, but it was satisfactory. I had to "board round" — that is, live a week at a place among the patrons of the school, and the boarding places were not always pleasant, but the experience was interesting, and when the three months were past, I was engaged for another month, and, this being accomplished, I took passage on the canal for home, this time on a packet boat. This was a boat built only for passengers, and was permitted to move as fast as the team would trot.

The Ohio Canal was at that time thought to be full of miasmatic vapors, and with good reason — as I found to my sorrow. When I arrived at home I had a well developed case of malarial fever that kept me in bed for many a long day. When I began to recover I arranged with my elder brother, Charles, to join in the purchase of an outfit for traveling, to wit, a horse and strong buggy to carry us to the southern states somewhere, to try to engage in teaching school. While I was yet bedridden we had everything arranged, and, on the fourth day after I was able to sit up, we started on our travel southward from our home in Johnstown, Licking County, and crossed the Ohio River into Kentucky, at Maysville, by what route I have no recollection, as I was very weak, and indifferent to all things. Maysville, I remember, and Paris, and Lexington, and Nashville, Tennessee, and Florence, Alabama, where we crossed the Tennessee River. Not far from this we saw some wonderful springs coming out from the mountain, the volume of water so large and strong as to afford a valuable waterpower. Then we turned to the west, toward the Mississippi River, intending to sell our horse and buggy at Memphis, and go home by the river if we did not get employment. . . .

III

Farming and College

I secured a place teaching in Mississippi. My school was successful, and at the close of my engagement I was urged to remain, but
asked to be excused, as I was going to enter college. Waiting for
my brother, whose term was not quite finished, I employed the
time in hunting. The days were getting long, and hot at midday,
and, on one occasion, having wounded a deer, I pursued it, with
others, through a cypress bayou, and, riding from the hot uplands,
dripping with perspiration, into and through this valley of death,
gave me a shock that laid me out on a log, to have a fearful con-
gestive chill. I was helped back to my office building, and put to
bed, and Dr. Davis was sent for, who dosed me with quinine and
calomel, in heroic doses, the effects of which are singing in my
ears today. . . .

I had no more chills, and was soon able to travel in a carriage
to Holly Springs, and to Memphis, where, with my brother, I took
passage on a steamboat for home. We left the steamboat at Ports-
mouth on the Ohio River, to take a canal boat for Newark, the
county seat of our home county. From Newark to Johnstown (our
home town) was twenty miles, and there was no public conveyance.
We stored our baggage, and started to walk home. We were over-
taken by a farmer who had been to market his grain, and obtained
a ride home in his wagon.

Newark was the market-place of the county, and a poor market
it was. The farmers were at the mercy of the traders, and, although
there was nominal competition with buyers, it was managed so
that the trader always had more profit from a bushel of grain than
the farmer who raised it. I have known wheat to be hauled twenty-

five miles, and dumped into the canal, because the farmer would rather do that than take the twelve and a half cents offered for it. Forty cents was considered a fair price for the best winter wheat, and eighteen cents for corn and oats. The demand for corn was regular at Newark, as there was a distillery there.

The fertile land of Ohio gave ample returns to the farmer for his labor, but the problem of transportation was then, as now, of the utmost importance. The little canal ditches dug through the country were believed, before and during construction, to be a sufficient means of transportation for many years, and perhaps for all time, but were insufficient from the time the first boat was placed in the water. Railroads were a necessity; they came, and took the business, and the old slow canals were abandoned. The wonderful forests of deciduous trees that covered the state of Ohio at that time, furnished material for the best white oak barrels in which corn, (as whiskey), and pork, and beef, were readily and safely sent to market, to eastern and southern ports.

A farmer's life was at that time, as it is now, a life of constant labor, and of stringent economy, if it was to be successful; and while it was more independent than any other, it was also more lonely. At the time of my youth, the conveniences for doing farm work were of the scantiest. The bull plow, with its wooden mold board, had not yet been driven out by the cast iron plow. Hoes, which were heavy, clumsy blades of iron, with an eye, through which a rough handle, cut from a brush patch or from a tree, and dressed down with axe and knife, were introduced, and they were a burden to work with — very much more tiresome than the light steel crook-necked hoes, attached to the light, smooth, turned ash handles of today. Harrows were made of logs hewed flat, and pinned together, furnished with iron teeth when they could be obtained, which was not always. These, with other farm tools, were freely loaned from neighbor to neighbor. Oftentimes the small grain had to be covered by a brush harrow. The grain was cut with a sickle, as by the earliest peoples, but the grain cradle was being introduced, and was a great improvement, and, in upstanding grain, was capable of cutting four acres a day in able and skillful hands. I was efficient with the cradle, the scythe, and the pitchfork, and liked to pitch bundles up to the stackers, or into the barn. Working with the hoe I heartily detested — it was such a clumsy, fatiguing thing.

While the implements of the farmer were of the rudest kind the fresh generous soil gave ample returns for the labor of cultivation; one hundred bushels of corn, thirty to forty bushels of wheat, sixty to eighty bushels of oats, and three hundred bushels of potatoes to the acre were usual yields. Farm life meant work of the most exacting character. The land must be cleared of timber, and all the logs that would split made into rails, which, laid up in a zig-zag manner, made our fences, the height of which was regulated by law, eight rails, stake-and-ridered, being a lawful fence to protect against unruly cattle. Many black walnut trees were made into rails on my father's farm which, had they been left standing until the present time, would be a fortune to the owner of the farm. There was no demand then for walnut lumber; the logs would not burn, the stumps would not rot, and were difficult to remove.

We had a large number of sugar-maple trees on the land, which were tapped in the spring of the year by boring an auger hole a few inches deep in the tree, and driving in a spout, made from elder, or other pithy limb. The pith, when punched out, left a channel for the sap, which was received in wooden troughs dug with an axe from butternut, ash, poplar, or linden trees — any soft wood that would not color or give a taste to the sap. A bark or board-covered camp was made in the forest, and a battery of iron kettles, each holding twenty or thirty gallons, were set in a row on a furnace made of such rough stones as could be picked up on the surface of the ground. Or the furnace was made of clay sides, banked up, and the kettles hung from a cross support of wood. The fires were kept burning during the sap season, night and day. In this way was made the sugar and molasses for family use, and for trade at the stores for such things as were necessary. It was not very hard work to make maple sugar, and it was interesting to see the sap of the maple converted into that desirable sweet substance.

When, in process of boiling, enough thick molasses had been accumulated to "sugar off" a kettleful, the careful final clarifying with eggs and milk, and boiling to the right density for granulation, was entrusted to experienced persons only. The neighboring young folk were notified, for this was one of the occasions for fun and jollity, and for a more intimate acquaintance among them. Another was the apple-butter stirring in the fall of the year, when the ripe fruit was made into cider, and the thick mass called apple butter. The cider was boiled down — five barrels into one, if I re-member rightly. A large copper kettle was hung over an open fire and into this the cut apples were introduced as fast as they could be mashed up by the stirrer, which was kept constantly in motion by one of the young people — who changed places when the work became too warm. The stirrer was a flat piece of board about an inch thick, and about three feet long, one end rounded to fit the curve of the bottom of the kettle, and with a hole bored through the other end, in which was inserted a long handle, which allowed the person stirring to stand some distance from the fire. The mak-ing of half a barrel of apple butter (one boiling, or kettleful), would frequently take until midnight.

The corn husking bees were also sources of amusement and friendly help. The corn was gathered by pulling it from the stand-ing stalk in the field, piled in great heaps in the barn, or in ridges on the ground, and the huskers would range in each side, contest-ing for the largest number of bushels. There was a rule that the lad finding a red ear was entitled to kiss the girl next him, or the girl of his choice. Quilting parties and spinning bees also made for friendly intercourse; among the men, the log rollings were neces-sary gatherings to help some settler who had cut down the timber on a piece of land, cut the logs into convenient lengths for burn-ing, and piled and burned the brush, but who needed help to pile the logs for burning. The neighbors would turn out and assemble with teams and chains to gather and pile the logs in great heaps ready for the fire.

A small flock of sheep and a few acres of flax were necessary to furnish a farmer's family with clothing. The flax was pulled, tied in small bundles, stood up in little shocks and left for the sun to dry the seed-heads. After threshed, it was spread thinly in the meadow, exposed to the dampness of dews and rain, until the stalks became brittle. Then it was gathered up and put away for winter's work with the breaking machine, the scutch board and hackle, to fit it for the spinning wheel and loom, and was finally woven into shirting or toweling. The breaking machines were all made on the farm with the axe, auger, and draw-shave.

The wool — necessary to furnish blankets and warm clothing — was washed, carded, spun and woven on the farm. It was also colored, cut, and made into various garments. My mother was above the average height of women, very ingenious, and very industrious, as it was necessary that she should be to bring up a family of nine children on a farm on the frontier of Ohio in the early years of the nineteenth century. She was noted in her youth for her beauty, and for the lovely, unselfish disposition which she maintained through all the vicissitudes of her long life, and which endeared her to all who had the privilege of her acquaintance.

My father was a man of medium height, the only child of indulgent parents, of excellent disposition and character, religiously disposed, an advocate of temperance, and a deacon in the Presbyterian Church. In youth he was sent to Gallipolis, to clerk in the store of one Bureau, and learn the business of a merchant. He was not a money maker, either as a merchant or a farmer. Life on the farm was not attractive to my parents or to any of their children, and we all left it as soon as possible.

My brother Charles and I had brought home enough money from our Mississippi venture to pay our way in college. He chose to enter a Presbyterian college at Marietta, while I preferred an Episcopal institution at Gambier. I told my father that as I had heard the Presbyterian side all my life, I desired to hear the Episcopal side.

I entered the freshman class at Kenyon College in A.D. 1844, having to make up some studies — Greek and Latin probably. I remember a fellow student from New York, George Brewerton, who was also "in the vocative," as we were said to be, who had a passion for painting, and gave so much attention to his paints and brushes that he could not keep up in his classes, and his parents had to recall him. Afterwards he became somewhat distinguished as an artist. My college life at Kenyon was that of the ordinary student of restricted means — which was the financial condition of nearly all the students. Part of the time I furnished my own food, and ate it in my room. I had some cooking done by a woman who lived near the college. She would roast a fowl or bake a pudding, or boil a ham for a small sum. I bought bread of the baker, and dressed fowls of a farmer's wife for what is now a very small price. I paid only twelve cents for a chicken, and eighteen cents for a small turkey. Other food prices were in proportion.

There were two secret societies in Kenyon at that time, the Philomathesian and the Nu Pi Kapa. They were rivals, of course, and the Nu Pi Kapa was the smaller, and was said to be southern in sentiment. It became so weak that it was necessary to draft members from the Philomathesian to maintain the organization. I was a member of the Philomathesian. My classmates were agreeable companions, generally working earnestly to acquire knowledge, and acquit themselves well. One, William King Rogers, became my most intimate friend, not only through our college life, but until his death. He was a character altogether lovely and honorable, became a lawyer of ability, and private secretary to President Hayes, with whom he had been in partnership in the practice of law in Cincinnati.

My standing in my class was such that I was awarded the honor of the Greek oration at the time of graduation. It may be that I knew some Greek at that time, but now I am ignorant of even the letters of the alphabet, and I regard my study of that tongue as a waste of time, and regret I had not applied myself to acquiring a knowledge of living languages. French, German, and Spanish would have been of some use to me in the practical business of life.

Toward the end of my college course, in my senior year, occurred a picnic to the Caves, a romantic place a few miles from the college, much frequented by pleasure parties, at which picnic I met Miss Mary E. Bronson, who was destined to be to me the chiefest blessing a man may hope for — a loving wife, devoted to the welfare of the family and the children of whom she was the mother, and to whom she bequeathed many of her admirable traits of character. . . .

My parents lived near Johnstown, about thirty miles distant from Gambier, and I frequently made the journey on foot, taking a luncheon of dates, when I could get them. I had read of the Arabs traveling long distances with only dates for food, and I tried and found them satisfactory. It was a pleasant four years that I spent in Kenyon, and at the close I had been entered as a student of law, (November 29 A.D. 1847) in the law office of Delano and Smith, in Mt. Vernon, Ohio, where my fiancée lived.

IV

Frontier Travel and Henry Clay

On October 3, 1848, I went to Cincinnati, to engage in the service of Henry Derby and Company, booksellers and publishers, as their agent to travel through the western states, to look after their interests, introduce their publications, and visit their customers. This firm was interested in the national series of school books published by A. S. Barnes and Company. In this business I visited the western and southwestern states industriously during the winter of 1848 and the spring and summer of 1849, and up to December '49. My first efforts were directed to the Kentucky schools, and I assisted Mr. Derby in the capitol of Kentucky, Frankfort, where the legislature was in session, and where he hoped to obtain an order for Kentucky lawbooks, which he published. This we found impossible during that session, as the members were engaged in a political wrangle that absorbed all of their time and attention. We had rooms at the largest hotel, where the majority of the members seemed to be quartered, and remained there a week or ten days, which was as long as we could endure the bad fare and general disorder. . . .

While in Lexington, I felt a strong desire to see the great orator, Henry Clay, the idol of the Whig party to which my father and all of my people belonged. I went to his residence and asked the servant if Mr. Clay was receiving visitors who only called to pay their respects — but I may as well extract from my diary the entry written at this time — in December, about the 15th, 1848.

"Called yesterday on the Hon. Henry Clay. His house is surrounded by trees, and is approached through a long winding avenue of evergreens. I was ushered in by his servant Charley.

A spare man, with hair thin and white, and a pale countenance, was reclining in an easy chair by an open fire. No one could mistake him. As I bowed myself into the room his face seemed to ask the reason of this call. I said 'I beg your pardon for this intrusion — I am a stranger, sir, and could not pass by your house a third time without calling to offer the humble tribute of my respect.'

'I thank you, sir' — rising very feebly, and offering me his hand cordially — 'I am just recovering from a severe sickness — you see me quite feeble', and he sat down again. 'Where do you reside, sir?'

'Ohio is my native state. Part of my life has been spent in Lancaster.'

'Your legislature seems to be in difficulty — indeed it seems to be of quite a serious character. Have you heard anything recently from Columbus?'

'Yes, sir, a message from there yesterday says there seems but little hope of an organization.'

"We talked of Olds, Medary, Ewing, Medill, of Kenyon College, McIlvaine, Chase, of education and schools. I said the most thorough school for females that I had any knowledge of was the Seminary of Monticello in Illinois; that the course was equal to any college course, and embraced the classics, and mathematics. He said he saw no propriety and no use in requiring the dead languages of ladies. A knowledge of their mother tongue, and of French, Spanish, and Italian, if they chose, was quite sufficient. His opinion was, and always had been, that it was a question with the boys whether they should be taught Latin and Greek. If they commenced their education early in life, and could always continue in school until grown, it was well enough to give them a thorough course in the classics, but if they commenced at fourteen or fifteen years of age, there were other things to which they could turn their attention to better advantage.

'Do you think such knowledge is necessary to a high attainment in eloquence?' I asked him.

'No, not particularly so.'

'Well, sir,' I said, 'you know that we students learn and recite from your speeches, and from those of other great orators, and try to catch the spirit, but that is not eloquence. Can you tell me wherein the secret lies — what course will lead to the highest of excellence?'

'Why, my dear friend,' he said — with an affectionate tone and smile I will never forget — 'eloquence is a very simple matter. If a man has person and voice, understands his subject thoroughly, and is in earnest, he cannot fail of being eloquent. And yet, it is something that must be sought after industriously; nature must be tutored. Look at the greatest of orators, for example.' Then he spoke of Richard Henry Lee, and Patrick Henry. He had heard Henry in his boyhood. One of his peculiarities was the perfect command of the muscles of his face. He could look with as much force as he could speak.

"Then, after some desultory conversation, I feared that, being feeble, I might weary him, and rose to take my leave. He asked that I would excuse him from accompanying me to the door, as he was afraid of the damp, misty air. It was a drizzly, murky day. I should have mentioned that soon after coming in I took a glass of wine with him." . . .

During my travels in the book business I was in Nashville, Tennessee, where General Zachary Taylor was passing through to assume his official duties as President. There was much crowding and pushing about the hotel, and I saw one well dressed man, of middle age, very drunk, who had followed General Taylor to his room, and from his room to the street, where the General was trying to avoid him by walking up and down the pavement, but the man pursued him, and tried to stop his walking, whereupon the General seized him by the shoulders, and turning him around, booted him into the street, exclaiming: "Now, damn you, maybe you'll let me alone, and some of your friends will take care of you — if you have any!" . . .

In the prosecution of my business I was at Florence, Alabama and found it necessary to go to Murfreesboro, by stagecoach. It was a Concord coach, hung on straps, over braced steel springs, and I was the only passenger. The driver was crazy from liquor and inate deviltry. The roads were in very bad condition, and part of the way lay up the dry bed of a mountain stream, covered with rolling stones, the driver urged his team to the utmost speed at every rough place, yelling and shouting: "Now you'll catch it — hold fast or I'll throw you out of the coach!" I was thrown from one side of the coach to the other, and up against the roof; my silk hat was crushed, and I was so beaten and bruised that I had to keep my bed for some days after my arrival at Murfreesboro.

Another memorable ride I had in Tennessee was from Pulaski to Memphis, March 6th and 7th, 1849. The condition of the roads was such that they could not send a coach through, but the mail contract required that the mail bags must go without delay, so they were strapped on the fore axle, hounds detached from the coach, some boards fastened on the mail bags, and corded fast, and on these the driver and myself, with four horses, started to cross the sea of mud between Pulaski and Memphis. The next time I encountered this road was in December, 1864, when I was chief quartermaster of the army of General Thomas, then in pursuit of Hood. I rode out of Pulaski on horseback, but, after a mile of examination, rode back and reported to General Thomas that it was impossible for the army to pursue the enemy any farther. The mud had been stiffened by the cold weather, and Hood's army had escaped on hard frozen ground, which thawed during the night, and prevented further pursuit.

In the spring of 1849 I was a passenger on a steamer from St. Louis to St. Joseph, Missouri, with a crowd of people, mostly Kentuckians, going to make homes on the Platte purchase, a tract of very fertile land recently acquired by the government from the Indians; also a number of passengers going to California, attracted by the report of the discovery of gold. Had I not been engaged in the book business, I would surely have been a forty-niner. The temptation was great. The Kentuckians who were to become settlers on the Platte lands were a merry, intelligent people, apparently all well off as to means, and the emigrants going to California were of the same middle class of American people, desirable citizens anywhere. St. Joseph was a town of but one street, on the bank of the restless Missouri River, which, not long after I was there, changed its channel, and washed the town site into the river bottom.

There was nothing to do in that frontier town, and I returned on the Mandan down the river to Booneville, where there was a lively growing town, with several schools. I was much pleased with Booneville and the country adjoining, and thought it would be a good place for me to settle. From Booneville I went to the capital of the state, and while there was shown specimens of cannel coal, taken from a mine on the north side of the river, in which the vein was said to be forty feet thick. This I had the curiosity to visit and examine, and I concluded that it was only a pocket, not a permanent vein. I visited several towns and schools in northern Missouri, and crossing the river at St. Charles, returned to St. Louis, where I interviewed all the teachers in the public and private schools.

From St. Louis, I went across Illinois to Peoria, and from Peoria crossed back to Quincy in a stage coach having nine passengers inside — three on a seat. My vis-a-vis in this coach was a young and witty Irishman, and we had a merry time crossing the endless prairies of Illinois. I was wearing a pair of large buffalo overshoes, and in order to change my position, I brought one of my feet up from between his knees, whereat he looked at it, and said, "Ye got in airly at the dishtribution of the feet," in such a comical, sympathizing tone of voice that the passengers roared with laughter, while he wore a face of injured innocence. He was kind-hearted, for, suspecting, for some reason, that I was out of money (and I was), he quietly offered to lend me some; but I did not need to borrow, as I had money at Quincy.

From Quincy I returned to St. Louis, and took up my conference with the school teachers. St. Louis, was, at this time, as it had been for many years, the center of the fur trade, and the trade with Santa Fé, and was growing rapidly, but land on the south side, toward Veitbush, was offered me at one hundred dollars an acre that is now covered with business blocks and fine residences. I returned to Cincinnati by steamer, and reported transactions, settled my accounts, and followed my fiancée and her father to Boston in the winter of '49 and '50, stopping, however, at Columbus, where the Supreme Court was in session, and where my schoolmate, John Sherman, was attending court. He applied for me to the judge to appoint a committee to examine me for admission to the bar. I was duly examined and regularly admitted to practice as an attorney and counselor at law, and solicitor and counselor in chancery, in any court of record in the state of Ohio. My winter was spent, nominally, in reading law in Boston. The celebrated trial of Professor Webster, for the murder of Parkman, was held in the courthouse there that season, and I attended it from beginning to end. . . .

I left Boston for the west in the spring of the year, intending to settle at Booneville, Missouri, open a law office, and make a home. I arranged with Barnes and Company, at 51, John Street, for a stock of books and stationery, which was sold me on credit.

At Cincinnati I called on my former employer, H. W. Derby, and after a sufficient visit, walked down Main Street on my way to the boat landing, when I began to feel dizzy. The houses assumed curious positions, and suddenly some one put his arm around me, and said: "Why, Bill, what's the matter with you? Have you been drinking?"

I said, indignantly, "No, John Miner, you know I never drink whiskey. I'm feeling queer — dizzy — I don't know what's the matter."

He looked at my finger nails. "Blue," he exclaimed, "you have the beginning of cholera; come with me," and he hurried me across to a grocery house — Allison Owen was the name over the door. Being inside he called to the clerk to hand down a bottle of brandy, and he poured out a half tumbler full, and, putting it to my lips, said: "Drink that, quick," then had someone call a carriage, put me in, and took me out to his home on Walnut Hills, high, above the city, and there gave me such remedies as he had in the house. After a few days, having recovered, I was about to resume my journey to Booneville, but Cousin John said: "You must not go there; they have cholera in St. Louis worse than we have here."

"Where shall I go, John?" I asked. "I want to be on the frontier somewhere."

"Go up the Mississippi, then," he answered. "There is a new territory, Minnesota — the capital is called St. Paul. You can get there by going to Chicago, and across Illinois to Galena, and from there by boat to St. Paul."

Accepting his advice I went to Chicago, how — whether on foot or horseback, or by the lakes, or by rail, I have not now the slightest recollection, but a letter I wrote June 28th says: "I will be in Chicago tomorrow night! From there to Galena is one hundred and fifty miles (part rail, and part coach), and from there are steam packet-boats that run the year round, except in winter. I expect to cross Lake Erie tomorrow on the steamer Arrow to Detroit, then by rail to Chicago."

I did cross on the Arrow — Capt. Arthur Edwards, — and years after met this same Edwards as captain and assistant quartermaster at Bridgeport, Alabama, where he was in charge of building boats.

I have no recollection of this journey until my arrival at Chicago, where the mud was so deep in the streets that it was heavy pulling for four horses to draw the coach to the Sherman House, and a plank was put out to enable the passengers to get from the coach to the door of the hotel.

I do not remember how I got to Galena; I think there was a cheap strap iron railroad from Chicago to Rockford, and a stage coach from there to Galena. At Galena I found a steamboat billed for St. Paul, the Ben Franklin. I was delighted with the passage up the beautiful river, and remained on deck from early morning until nightfall. I recovered my health and spirits, and landed at the foot of Jackson Street, St. Paul, on the 5th of July, A.D. 1850. . . .

V

Westward to Minnesota Territory

I found St. Paul to be a straggling frontier town, scattered over a narrow bench of land, ninety feet or so above the river — nearly all on Third Street. Henry Jackson, Louis Robert, John E. Irvine, and some others whose names do not occur to me, had squatted, and made claim to patches of land lying around a little log hut, erected on the bank of the river, by order of a priest of the Catholic Church, Father Gaultier, for a confessional, and for other purposes of the missionary. He told me that, having occasion to publish the marriage notice of Vitale Guerin, he had to select a name for the chapel, and, remembering that Saint Anthony, Saint Peter, and Saint Croix had been honored in the neighborhood, he thought he would give it the name of Saint Paul.

There was a long, narrow frame building, "Central House," used as a hotel and meeting place for the Governor's council, and the first courts. The hotel was kept by Robert Kennedy, and I engaged a room and board therein. After looking the place over, and finding a little frame building, twelve feet by twenty-four, on the corner of Third and Robert Streets — rent nine dollars a month — I put out my sign, "W. G. Le Duc, Attorney at Law," and waited for such business as might offer.

A few days after my arrival, I was walking along the bluff, after breakfast, with a large, hearty lumberman, who had stopped at the hotel overnight, and who seemed in gay good humor, when he suddenly stopped, on seeing a number of logs floating down the river, and exclaimed: "See the logs! What mark is that on them? That's my mark — they are my logs — my God — the boom has broke — and I am a ruined man!" He went back to the hotel, and was dead before night — of cholera, the doctors said. . . .

On the 22nd of July the steamer Yankee, a small stern-wheel boat, one of a number of small steamers engaged in the river trade between Galena and St. Paul, was chartered to explore the Minnesota, or, as it was then called, the St. Peter River. The boat was crowded with people who were desirous of a knowledge of the fertile Minnesota valley, knowing that it must soon be opened for the frontier settler. The passengers were mostly men, but there were enough women to make up cotillion sets, and we anticipated a merry time.

The clergy were represented by the Reverend Edward Duffield Neill, a Presbyterian missionary; the medical fraternity by Doctor Potts; statesmen by a gentleman who had been an aid to General Harrison and later our minister to Russia; another member of the party was a graduate of West Point, and another of the Yale Law School; another, one of the Renvilles, had been interpreter for Nicollet; another was an Indian trader, Joe La Framboise, who was returning to his station on the Cottonwood, a branch of the St. Peter's. He was noted for his linguistic attainments, and could acquire any Indian language with a few days opportunity it was said. He certainly was proficient in English and French, and spoke both with remarkable fluency and elegance. Another well known frontier character was a Winnebago halfbreed, Baptiste, whose Indian dress and habits attracted much attention for a time.

As we entered the current of the St. Peter, at Mendota, the stream was nearly bank full, and it seemed like navigating a sluggish canal. Arriving at the Indian village of old Shakopee, the boat landed and attracted a great crowd including the chief himself, who demanded toll in return for his permission to navigate the waters beyond his village. The traders, after some pow-wow, and distribution of presents — and I think a little whiskey — quieted the old fellow, and we proceeded up the river to Traverse des Sioux, where there was a mission station, in charge of a Mr. Hopkins, if I remember aright. Here the Captain bought a lot of wood and old rails, and we next landed at Belle Prairie, and, while the steamboat hands were getting wood, attempted to have a dance on the prairie grass. Our next landing was at Mankato, the mouth of the Blue Earth River, and while the firemen were cutting some of the young ash trees for fuel, we rambled around on the shores. I picked up a piece of lignite coal, weighing three or four pounds, and brought it to St. Paul, where I had it on exhibition, and from it inferred that a vein of lignite must exist somewhere along the river. (In the year 1868 or '69 I was in the country somewhere half way between the Blue Earth River and Bigstone Lake, and I saw an exposure of lignite that seemed about ten feet thick, from which I believe that specimen had originated.)

Leaving this landing we pushed on slowly upstream, trying to reach La Framboise trading-post on the Cottonwood, but found it necessary to tie up to the bank, and cut more wood. The day was oppressively hot, the firemen were exhausted and night was approaching. The boat was made fast to the trees growing on the bank, and the captain announced that in the morning he would turn down-stream. Millions of mosquitos invaded the boat. Sleep was impossible. A smudge was made in the cabin but brought little relief. Some — I among others — were ferried across the river, and, making our way through the tall grass of the bottom land, we climbed the high bluffs, where the wind had a chance to blow, and we got a few hours rest on the short buffalo grass. The next morning we were all ready and anxious to leave the place, and return to St. Paul. When we started, I stationed myself on the upper deck with a compass and watch, and tried to map the channel of the river. While not accurate, the result was approximately correct, and it was turned over to a map maker, and published in my year book of 1853. We arrived at St. Paul the evening of the 26th of July, and had had no accidents to mar our expedition.

Some time during the summer I had occasion to go to St. Anthony, a village of a few houses on the east side of the Mississippi at the falls; I crossed the river above the falls, in a birch bark canoe. The man who took me over was named Tapper, and he was afterward ferryman for many years. I went down to examine the old government sawmill, and noticed the place where the rock of the falls had broken down. The fresh break being very apparent, I measured it, and found a retrocession of the falls, of ninety feet, which seemed very astonishing until examination showed a very soft sandstone, and underlying the limestone cap rock. I called attention to this in my year book for A.D. 1851. How to prevent the falls of St. Anthony from becoming a mere rapid, became an important problem, which was not solved until the army engineers were given the task by the War Department. A tunnel was run in, under the limestone, and a dam of supporting granite sustains and will preserve the falls indefinitely.

The Secretary of the Territory for some reason made himself very unpopular with the legislative powers, and some of the members came to me and suggested that I keep a supply of stationery, such as would be required for the members during the session. I told them that I had a stock of books and stationery coming, and intended to have a bookstore, with all things necessary, and keep it up. I hired a little frame house of Louis Robert, on the corner of Third and Robert Streets, on the opposite corner from my office, and opened a bookstore when the little stock of goods arrived sometime during the fall of the year 1850. This gave me a living profit from the start, for there was a demand for such articles, not only in the growing territory, but also in the government forts, Snelling, Ripley, and Ridgely, and some lumber camps. When the Territorial Legislature met the members were well pleased to find a book store, and gave me all the public patronage they could.

One night four members came in. David Olmsted, being the spokesman, inquired if I had playing cards, and if I would permit them to play a game of rounce. I did not know what rounce was, but I had the cards, and a place to play at their service. David Olmsted said: "What shall the rounce be?"

"Webster's Unabridged," said one. This work had just been issued, and I had a few copies, at five dollars a copy, and the first rounce was for a Webster's Unabridged. The game was popular with those members who avoided the whiskey shops, and before the end of the session my shelves were cleared of all except school books.

I bought a house and lot at the corner of Third and Wabasha Streets, of Vital Guerin, for nine hundred dollars — three hundred cash, and the balance payable in one and two years. The house was a log structure. The ground floor had a living room and two bedrooms when divided and plastered. There was also a kitchen and a floor overhead, which made a storage room. Alongside I built a store room, sufficient for the bookstore. To this very modest but comfortable home in the spring of the next year — 1851 — I introduced my bride — a great remove from her mother's handsome house in Mt. Vernon, Ohio, where, an only daughter, she was surrounded by comfort and all the elegancies of civilized life usual in a little city in the interior of Ohio, which she gave up cheerfully to begin here the founding of a home of her own, and a married life of fifty-three years of unclouded happiness.

The Governor's house was not very much better than mine. It was situated on Third Street, on the south side, between Jackson and Robert, a story and a half frame house, with a porch on the east side. Among the people I think of in St. Paul at this time there were besides Governor Ramsey and his family, and the Reverend Edward Duffield Neill and his wife, Henry M. Rice, and Edmund Rice, George L. Becker. There was Doctor Potts, and also Doctor Borup, an educated Dane, who was in the employ of the American Fur Company, and Charles Oakes, a Yankee, who was in partnership with Borup. They had married sisters, two half-breed Chippewa girls, whose father had sent them to an eastern school. They were very pleasant people — socially successful.

The winter of 1850–51 having passed without a thaw from November first to the middle of March, the Reverend E. D. Neill, John McCloud and myself, wishing to go east, joined one John Rogers who was going to Prairie Du Chien to get a sled-load of groceries. The first day we went on the ice to Red Rock, and then across the prairie to Point Douglas, where we stopped the first night at a tavern kept by David Barker. From Point Douglas we went across the river, and down Prairie Island through the timber to Red Wing, and from there to the foot of Lake Pepin, where we slept in the house of a trader. The next day's journey was across Lake Pepin, and we found a place to sleep at a trader's camp. The next day we followed the prints of the mail carrier's horse on the ice, which was bare of snow. We had to drive in the night, and were late in reaching a house. I was in advance, feeling for the prints of the mail carrier's horse with my moccasined feet, and of course it was slow traveling. Finally we saw a light on the shore, and Neill and McCloud both insisted that we should drive toward the light. I insisted the driver should follow the mail carrier's tracks, which seemed to lead away from the light. We finally stopped and shouted until a man appeared on the shore and called back to us not to try to cross, for there was a long air hole, but wait until he made a torch, and lighted us around it. This he did. His camp was where is now Trimbelle. He could furnish food and lodging (on the floor) and we made an early start in the morning, and got safely to Prairie Du Chien, where we found coaches to Chicago, and from there we went to Detroit by the Michigan Southern, and by a Canadian coach to Niagara Falls, and then to New York over the Central Railroad.

Having purchased stock from A. S. Barnes and Company, and from Harper Brothers, and Appleton, I went to Middletown, Connecticut, to see my grandmother's sister, Clarissa Sumner, who was the last of the family of Colonel John Sumner to leave their native town for the west. Taking her with me, I hastened to Johnstown, Ohio, the home of my parents, where I left her with my family, going from there to Mt. Vernon, Ohio, to be married to Miss Mary Elizabeth Bronson. We were married in traveling clothes, and started at once for Columbus and Cincinnati, and went by way of the Ohio and Mississippi Rivers to St. Paul — our home. It was a long wedding trip, mostly by water, on the comfortable river steamers of that day.

On our journey up the river from St. Louis, we made the acquaintance of the Honorable Henry H. Sibley and his wife, with whom a warm friendship continued through life. The Sibleys lived at Mendota, which was and had been for many years the headquarters of the American Fur Company in Minnesota, with Mr. Sibley in command. He had governed with wisdom and justice. His word was law, and his signature to an obligation for money was as good as gold. He was a great sportsman, and we occasionally found time to hunt together, and our families exchanged friendly visits until after the death of Mrs. Sibley.

My bookstore was prosperous, and I started my brother Joseph in the same business in St. Anthony. In the year 1853, I brought some pianos to St. Paul. The first one sold was to a Mrs. Presley, who was ambitious to own a piano although she was entirely ignorant of music. Her husband became wealthy, and she was very popular with the firemen of the city. Her kindness to the sick and poor made her many friends. I published year books, for the years 1851–2–3, advertising my business, and recording notable events, such as the Indian treaty, and giving names to some localities, one being the name of 'Minnesota' to the St. Peter River, and another 'Minnehaha' to what had been called Brown's Falls.

These little books are standard history for the very early territorial days of Minnesota, especially with regard to the Indian treaty, which I attended as a visitor, and to report for the New

York Tribune. There were about seven thousand Indians congregated on the treaty grounds, at Traverse des Sioux, all hungry, after the manner of Indians, and all willing to remain until the last beef of the drove was killed, and the last barrel of pork or flour issued. The weather was hot, and storms frequent — of almost daily occurrence — making the Indian camps so uncomfortable that they concluded something must be done for relief. A thunder bird dance was determined on.

Accordingly a pole, fifteen or twenty feet in height, was erected on a high place in the prairie, about a mile in the rear of the treaty arbor, and to the top was attached the thunder bird, a large bunch of feathers, and other light material, tied with a cord that allowed it to swing about freely in a lively breeze. Around the pole were two circles of Indians, as many as chose to engage in the dance, the inner circle of women, and the outer of men. At the base of the pole were the musicians, three in number, two with rattles made by tying rawhide on the end of a hand-piece containing gravel, and letting it harden, in bulbous form, and one beating a wolfskin, stretched over a hollow log. The dancing was nothing but a hopping up and down in time to the beat of the tom-tom.

After about a half hour of dancing the tom-tom beat more furiously, and, from behind a knoll on the prairie, came a single line of mounted enemies of the thunder bird, charging at a gallop. As they approached the pole the horses were urged to their fastest speed, and as each horseman passed the pole, he fired at the thunder bird, which was soon shot all to pieces, so that it hung dead against the pole. This with the feast that followed, ended the thunder bird dance, and the storms ceased, and fine fair weather prevailed until the breaking up of the encampment.

The winter of 1851–52 was very cold, but with a house warmed by Canadian heating stoves, and plenty of wood, we made ourselves comfortable, and celebrated Christmas and New Year's after the manner of our friends back in the states. Other young people in St. Paul were no better off than we were, and all were hopeful, young and happy, content with the life before us. Young and old officers from Fort Snelling, and occasionally from other military stations in the territory, added to the number of educated, intelligent people in our growing city. The profits of the book trade were large enough to defray the expenses of our economical housekeeping, and an occasional fee from my law practice was a welcome addition to our slender income. The increase in the demand for books, and for other things in my line of business, made it necessary to build a lean-to on the south side of my house, and on the north side I erected a two story frame building. This was built of good pine lumber, then to be had for little money. It was well put together, and eventually it was moved out on Wabasha Street, and afterward to other places, and is now on some side street.

During the session of the legislature I drew a charter for a railroad company to incorporate the Lake Superior and Mississippi Railroad Companies, and had it introduced by a St. Paul member, (Farrington, I think). The bill was passed, and the meeting for organization, if I remember correctly, was called to meet at my office. At this first meeting only Governor Ramsey and I were present, and we adjourned to meet one week from date. At this second meeting a quorum of the incorporators were present: Edmund Rice, George L. Becker, and also a Mr. Newton, from Superior or Duluth. He was the only one present who had any knowledge of railroads. We admitted him to the company, and were thankful for his advice.

I took a partner in the book trade — an accountant, D. Rohrer. In June I took my wife with me when I went to buy stock in New York, leaving her to visit her mother at Mt. Vernon, Ohio. Barnes and Company urged me to go to Cuba and New Orleans for them, and I agreed to go home by way of steamer to Havana, New Orleans and St. Louis, and shipped on very short notice on the steamer Ohio, arriving at Havana June 2nd, as appears from the following letter to my wife.

"Havana, June 2, 1852

"After a tedious voyage of seven days and twelve hours we arrived at this port yesterday morning. Expecting the vessel to sail at three o'clock, I employed the day exploring this most strange and old fashioned town.

"It is an entirely new world to me in vegetation, but very old in artificial adornment and culture. No one should think he understands Don Quixote, or The Three Spaniards, or the Moorish Hispano legends, until he has seen an old Spanish town. They are all alike, I am told. . . .

"I am sitting on the deck of our vessel with my paper on my

knee, under an awning, and the mercury at any height you like to imagine. A gentleman sitting opposite me is actually raining perspiration. We are looking — panting — sighing for the sea breeze which every morning is sure to bring, and, which alone makes this climate endurable. The water begins to dimple even now, and half an hour hence will probably fan us to dryness. This is a most beautiful harbor, and might be unequaled for comfort and security did the Spaniards know enough to improve it properly. But as it was by nature so it would be left by the Spaniards.

"We are anchored on the opposite side of the harbor from the city. On the hill above us is seen a part of Moro Castle, and the barracks of the soldiers are down along the shore. The cocoanut and palm trees, with their magnificent foliage, shade some of the houses, and the crows and negro scavengers are the most busy of any moving things before me. A group of soldiers, it is true, are parading out in front of one of the shanties — their houses deserve no better name. I will give you a description of one; one may answer for all, except that some are more expensive than others. They are of one story, generally, built of coral rock and cement plastered inside and out, the outside colored a dirty yellow or red or brown. They cover the earth with flag stones or cement, for a floor, which is sometimes painted and sometimes not. The doors of the houses are huge double planked barn-like doors — bolted planks, proof against an ordinary assault of musketry — and with a smaller door for ordinary family use, the larger being for the admission of horse and carriage. The windows are destitute of glass, but have a guard of iron rods outside, and shutters inside. The roofs are of tile.

"I was fortunate enough to have made the acquaintance, on the ship, of a merchant from New York, who spoke the language, and came to buy tobacco. He took me with him to various places, and thus I have had access to the wholesale dealers houses. The *volante* (the cab of Havana) is a two wheeled vehicle, with shafts twelve or fourteen feet long, drawn by a horse or mule, which is mounted by a Negro driver, who wears leather greaves from the knee to the foot, which is bare often, but always adorned with immense jingling spurs with rowels an inch long. The body of the volante is an old-fashioned gig body, hung upon leather straps in front of the axle tree, and seats two persons. My merchant friend took me in a volante to call on a wholesale dealer at his residence.

We entered at the small door, and, as we stepped inside, the family *volante* was in front of us to the right, in a large room with a circular table, on which was some bric-a-brac. On the walls were some religious pictures and emblems. The *volante* occupied one end of this room, and if run forward, would have passed through to the area, on which fronted the bedroom, kitchen — and dining room, if there was one — and the stable.

"The man we came to see was sitting near the entrance to the open area, at a desk, conversing with a customer. He asked us to be seated, and help ourselves to fruit. There was a table near, on which were grapes, oranges, and figs. We ate some fruit, and, after the customer departed, the planter took us into a large room, with shelves behind doors along one entire side. As he opened one of these doors numerous packages of tobacco were seen, all neatly labeled, and he took down certain ones for examination by my friend, when prices and terms were discussed, and memorandums made. The tobacco bought would be brought from the plantation where grown, and shipped as soon as the slow transportation of the country would permit. We took a drive to the Bishop's garden — a place of general resort — and were caught in a sudden shower.

"June 3rd, 1852. It is a beautiful morning, and the vessel, relieved from the crowd of passengers, goes through the water rejoicing. Those of us who are for New Orleans, being few in number, will probably have a pleasant time. We will meet the muddy waters of the Mississippi that show themselves far out in the gulf, sometime tomorrow; and we will be due in New Orleans the day after tomorrow. The time from Havana to New Orleans, in favorable weather, is sixty hours, New Orleans being, as you may remember, one hundred miles up the river.

"June 6th. Arrived in New Orleans yesterday afternoon. Have but little to do. May stop at Natchez, also at Memphis, and hope to find a letter from you at Keith and Woods, St. Louis. My visit to New Orleans was almost entirely useless, as the object for which I went was almost accomplished before I got there. I was glad to escape from that city as the cholera is there — prevalent, as also other diseases. You don't know how glad I am to get among old familiar places again. I think I am nearer 'old familiar faces.'

"I expect to remain at St. Louis one week at least, and stop at Keokuk, Rock Island, Davenport and Galena, then to St. Paul, where I am very much needed to look after our affairs, which, having arranged to leave safely in Rohrer's hands, I will leave for Ohio."

After stopping at St. Louis, and other places, in the interests of Barnes and Company, I arrived safely at St. Paul. My wife was in Mt. Vernon, Ohio, at this time, visiting her mother, with our first-born daughter, and remained there during the winter, and until I returned from the World's Fair — the Crystal Palace show — in New York, in the following year.

VI

The Crystal Palace Exhibition

Theodore Sedgewick, and a number of public spirited men, incited by the success of the London World's Fair inaugurated by Prince Albert, determined to rival his exhibition by a world's fair in New York City in the year 1853.* They erected on the west half of Reservoir Square, then "away up town" that beautiful structure of iron and glass known as the Crystal Palace of New York. This building, while inferior to the rectangular edifice erected for the London exposition, was, in symmetrical proportions and architectural beauty, far superior to anything that had been constructed of iron and glass. Filled with the choicest productions of industry and art from all parts of the world, the building was at length formally opened to the public — a dream of beauty and utility never to be forgotten by those fortunate enough to see it. Advertisements of the exhibition were widely circulated. In the winter of 1852–53 the once-a-week mail, carried up the river on the ice, brought one of these notices finally into my hands. At once I saw in the world's fair an opportunity to attract attention to our territory, then practically unknown, and to induce immigration to move in our direction.

After consulting Governor Ramsey, I prepared and had introduced into the territorial legislature, then in session, a bill providing for the appointment by the governor of a commissioner to the fair, and appropriating three hundred dollars for the preparation of an exhibit. The bill passed, and I was given the

* The material in this chapter was used by Le Duc in a paper he prepared for the Minnesota Historical Society in 1898. It was later published under the title "Minnesota at the Crystal Palace Exhibition, New York, 1853," in *Minnesota History*, 1:351–368 (August, 1916).

appointment. In the early spring I set about securing such an exhibit as would attract attention to Minnesota. At this time agriculture was practiced only in the gardens at the United States forts and on the farms of a small colony of Yankees who had settled on some fertile lands a few miles above the junction of the St. Croix with the Mississippi, called Cottage Grove. Here Joseph and Theodore Furber, James Norris, and Joseph Haskell were demonstrating the richness of the soil by raising with great success and profit large crops of all the small grains usually grown in northern latitudes: wheat, rye, oats, barley, and corn. The demands of the logging camps, of the Indian trading posts, and of the forts however, largely exceeded the amount of cereals produced. I secured samples of all the varieties grown.

My next visit was to the principal trading post of the American Fur Company, located at Mendota, which since 1834 had been under the management of Henry H. Sibley. He supplied me with specimens of the best furs in his possession, and gave me a letter to Ramsay Crooks, formerly president of the company, but at this time engaged in the fur commission business in New York, which was the means of placing at my disposal the finest furs in the world. At the suggestion of Henry M. Rice I accompanied his clerk E. A. C. Hatch on a trip to the trading posts on the upper Mississippi to get an Indian canoe and samples of wild rice, or manomin, as the Chippewas in their tongue called the *Zizania aquatica*, a plant bearing a grain of great food value to the Indians living among the marshy lakes of northern Minnesota and Wisconsin, and to any peoples who shall in the future live in those regions. The rice as well as a birch-bark canoe of the best pattern and other articles of Indian make I obtained through the courtesy of Mr. Russell, the factor in charge of the trading post of Borup and Oakes, and M. Cunradie, a gentlemanly, well-educated, competent clerk whom I had known in St. Paul, and who had been banished to this frontier post by his employers because of his persistent indulgence in whiskey and convivial frolics. Cunradie was a native of Alsace or Lorraine, and was a foster brother of Louis Napoleon, who had just carried out his successful coup d'état in France. Cunradie sought my assistance in getting to New York, saying in his broken English:

"Ah, my fren', eef I can only get back to France, my foster brother he will see I shall haf ze good place. I queet dese *sacré bleu* squaw camp an' come to Paree. I queet wat you call hell and get to heaven, ees it not so?"

"But, Cunradie, I have no money to pay clerk hire; only three hundred dollars for the entire business."

"Only t'ree hundred dollar for ze entire treep! *Mon Dieu*, but zat ees too leet' for ze whiskey beel of ze commish'."

As I was about to start on my return journey, Cunradie again appeared, and, taking me to a corral, said: "I show you wat will more attract ze peep' zan all canoe or fur or grain. You see zat fine buffalo bool? You put heem in your show and everybody shall say, 'Meenesota! W'ere ees zat?' Zen shall ze peep' mak' some inquire. I geef you heem, an' eef you get more zan hees cost, you geef me to go to France, eh, ees it not so?"

"Impossible, Cunradie, I could not tie him behind Mr. Hatch's buggy, and I can't drive him to St. Paul. Now if I had him at St. Paul when I start down the river, I might take him along and try to help you back to your beloved Paris, but you see that it is impossible."

"May be not imposs' eef I can get heem to St. Paul before you go."

I bade Cunradie good bye with no further thought of the matter. A week or ten days afterward, as I was sitting in my office in the building at the corner of Wabasha and Bench streets, over the post-office, in St. Paul, the door opened, and a softly moccasined footfall caused me to turn to the intruder, a solemn half-breed Chippewa, who announced in an undertone, "Mr. Cunradie have send buffalo bull."

"What! Buffalo bull! Oh, I hope not. Where is he?"

"See," he said briefly, pointing out of the window which overlooked Bridge Square. And there to my utter surprise and dismay was Cunradie's young bison, an iron ring in his nose, a rope attached to the ring, and the rope in the hands of a second half-breed. By them Cunradie had sent a letter claiming the fulfillment of my rash promise: that if the buffalo were on the spot when I started, I would take him.

And now my troubles began. The bull was hungry; the Indians were more hungry. After diligent inquiry I obtained the use of a stable belonging to Mr. Selby on St. Anthony Hill. In this building the bull was housed and properly fed, while the Indians were supplied with rations and given permission to sleep on the hay in the stable loft. There were not many children or young lads in St. Paul at that time, but what they lacked in numbers, they made up in activity of mind and body, and in curiosity. They visited the Selby stable in squads; and when the stolid half-breeds were absent or asleep, the children would tear the battens off or pry open the door in order to get a better view of the animal. They became so troublesome that at length I had the Indians take the bison out and lead him through the streets.

He was really a very handsome beast, between three and four years old; not so large through the shoulders as he would be later when his full growth was attained. His fine silky fur was jet black and glossy, though he was shaggy around the head, neck, and shoulders. His horns were short, sharp, black, and polished, and from out of the mass of shaggy locks adorning the front of his head gleamed a pair of black, piercing eyes that were ever on the alert, flashing the warning *noli me tangere*, "no familiarity allowed." His motions were quick and graceful. While lying at rest, he could spring at a bound to his feet, lower his head to meet an attack or charge an enemy with the suppleness of a cat. The buffalo bull in his prime, when angered, is to be feared by any wild beast in America. Horses, unless they are trained to the hunt or are otherwise accustomed to his presence, invariably bolt at the sight or smell of him.

Third Street was cleared of teams when the Indians led the bull down its length to the steamer "Ben Franklin," on the day of my departure. At the stern of the boat a place had been partitioned off with strong boards, and into this pen the animal was taken after much persuasion of various kinds. Here he was free to eat, drink, and sleep, with sufficient room in which to turn around. But except in the night he had scanty opportunity to rest. The roustabouts on the boat were men whose winters were spent in the woods in choppers' camps, where an opportunity to play practical jokes on each other, to tease any live creature, or to make a bet on anything or everything was never neglected. In similar fashion on this trip during their leisure time between landings, they were wont to amuse themselves by startling the bull with thrusts of a pole and in laying wagers as to how many such thrusts would make him mad enough to charge the side of his pen. The result of this form of amusement was apparent before we reached Galena. The approach of a deck hand was the signal for a flashing of the black eyes, a lowering of the pointed horns in so menacing a manner as to frighten any timid person away. It was clear to me that the sooner I parted company with Cunradie's buffalo, the better it would be for my peace of mind and for my limited appropriation. . . .

My attempts to sell the buffalo failed, and I hastened to make arrangements to get my exhibits aboard a steamer whose insistent bell was serving notice that it was to start for St. Louis immediately. After some difficulty the deck hands of both boats succeeded in transferring my buffalo to the down-river steamer, and I was on my way to St. Louis. The men employed on board were white men, the war not yet having turned the Negro loose for work on steamboats, and they varied the monotony of their rough life by constant investigation as to the agility and other peculiarities of the buffalo when disturbed by clubs and chunks of coal, all of which only increased his suspicions and irritability, and made the handling of him anything but a desirable task by the time the boat reached St. Louis. Fortunately we tied up alongside a steamer billed to start for Cincinnati within a few hours. I arranged for passage thereon and had my freight at once removed to the Ohio River boat, the usual provision being made for the bull. The problem of getting the latter into his new quarters presented the usual difficulties, since he refused to let any one get near enough to fasten a rope through the iron ring in his nose. Through strategy this was at length accomplished, and the bull was started toward the bow of the boat and the gangplank.

At this time the levee at St. Louis was paved with cobblestones. The water was rising rapidly, and the draymen were hurriedly engaged in removing from the steep bank the immense lots of freight that were piled too close to the mounting floods. Much of it appeared to be hogsheads of sugar from New Orleans; and the Irish draymen and their Negro helpers, the horses and mules, were all in a tangle of hurried confusion. When the buffalo came to the open gangway of the boat, he did not wait to go ashore dryshod on the gangplank, but jumped overboard into the muddy waters of the Missouri and swam off toward the bank, up which he clambered, blowing the water from his nostrils, shaking his shaggy head, and bellowing furiously. Horses and mules, dragging their empty or loaded drays, fled in a panic, with their drivers, no less frightened than themselves, shouting and urging them on.

The animals attached to unloaded drays became unmanagable, and the wildest confusion reigned. . . .

The captain told me he saw two casks [of sugar] get away from frightened stevedores and go to sweeten the yellow Missouri soup for the fishes. When the buffalo was safely on board and we were fairly out in the stream, the captain congratulated me and himself that we had gotten beyond the reach of legal processes which might have tied up his boat for a week.

We arrived at Cincinnati in due time. I had written to an old Kenyon College classmate, then engaged in the practice of law in that city, advising him of the date of my arrival and asking him to have some one meet me who would not be afraid to lead a buffalo bull across the city to the Miami freight station. The stalwart butcher who appeared at the landing looked the bull over and declined the job with decided promptness. He was willing to take reasonable chances with any ordinary bull, but no money would tempt him to risk himself with this ferocious-looking animal. My friend and I held a conference.

"He's not so wicked and dangerous as he looks, is he?"

"No, I think not. I believe he was tractable enough at home. His owner used to hitch him to a sled and make him draw wood and other things. But the treatment he has received at the hands of steamboat roustabouts has made him suspicious and unsociable, especially with strangers and in strange places."

"But he is used to you by this time, and you are not afraid of him? I don't think I can find anyone else to undertake the job."

"No, I'm not afraid of the beast, but I am afraid of seeing some of my acquaintances on the streets. I shouldn't care to meet Dick A — or Dan B — And then the girls! Besides I'll have to take the middle of the street."

"Oh, never mind that! I'll walk up with you. I think it hardly likely that we shall meet anyone we know at this time of day."

I turned into a shop and purchased a good ash hoe handle and had a spring snap large enough to take in the bull's nose ring attached to it. Thus equipped we started back to the levee. As we came in sight of the river we saw the steamer on which I had just arrived in midstream under a full head of steam, bound up-river. I was just congratulating myself that at last I was rid of Cunradie's bull, but my joy was premature and short-lived, for hitched to a steamboat ring half way up the levee was the buffalo, holding a reception for a respectful crowd of wharf rats. Arranging to have my goods sent to the Miami station, I hooked on to the buffalo with my hoe handle and started up Broadway. Approaching teams hastily turned into side streets and alleys; those following me declined to pass. The street was mine. My friend, after half a square, deserted me and betook himself to the sidewalk, where he attempted some witticisms at my expense with the passers-by. Fortunately I met no one who knew me. On arriving at the freight depot, I secured a car and saw my goods and livestock safely on board for Buffalo, whither I followed in a few hours. From Buffalo I was fortunately able to ship the car through without change to Albany. At Albany, however, it was necessary to have my freight hauled across the river, and, for the second time, I led the buffalo from one station to another, a distance of half a mile or more. On the bridge I was joined by a prospecting Yankee, with whom I fell into conversation.

"Goin' to the fair down to York with that there — that — it's a buffalo, ain't it?"

"Yes, it is a buffalo, and a very fine specimen of its kind."

"It is fur a fact, a derned cute-lookin' beast, slick as a mole, and spry as a cricket. Jeeminy, but he'd made a fine show! Side show, you know. Goin' to show him?"

"No, he is a part of the exhibit from Minnesota."

"Minnesoty! Where's that?"

"Up at the headwaters of the Mississippi River. Do you know where the Falls of St. Anthony are?"

"Oh, yes, my old Morse jography tells that. It's away out in the middle of the continent. Injun country, ain't it?"

"Yes, that is Minnesota territory now, and that is where this splendid specimen of the bison was caught and tamed."

"Bison? Bison?"

"Yes, that is the proper name for the animal, though it is commonly called buffalo."

"Do you want to sell him? I have a friend who is gettin' up a side show, and he would fit in like a bug in a rug. How much would you take fur him delivered down in York?"

"Has your friend the money to buy so fine an animal?"

"Yes, he's pretty well heeled, an' if he takes a fancy to a thing,

48

he pays cash down. If you'll tell me where you are goin' to put up down at the fair, we'll call on you fur a trade."

We had by this time reached the freight station, where my obliging acquaintance assisted me in getting the buffalo safely stowed away in his car. As he bade me good bye, he remarked, "But you didn't say 'bout how much you thought him wuth?"

"Considering the rarity and beauty of the animal, and the expense and trouble of his capture and transportation, he ought to bring three thousand dollars."

"Three thousand dollars! Well, that's a purty high figure fur any cud-chewin' beast. But he might pay interest on it if well showed. We'll have to think it over."

Arriving at New York on a Saturday afternoon, I engaged a room at the Astor House, and immediately set out to find a friend, Mr. S. A. R——, a member of a well-known publishing firm. I explained to him the nature of my business in New York; told him of the expected arrival of my exhibit by the night freight, and invited him to join me the next morning (Sunday) about ten o'clock and inspect the cargo. At the appointed time R—— appeared, dressed in elegant Sunday attire, six feet two inches in height, faultless in figure — the handsomest man in New York. We made our way to the freight depot on the river road, which was located on the west side near Canal Street. The car was standing in the yards, ready to be unloaded as soon as I could decide on what disposition to make of its contents. It was Sunday. The directors of the Crystal Palace could not be seen. What was to be done with the buffalo? He could not remain in the freight yards. R—— suggested that I hire someone to take him over to the Bull's Head stables, where he could be cared for until I could see the directors and have other quarters provided for him. His suggestion was adopted, except as to hiring some one to lead the bull across the city. This task I was again obliged to take upon myself. Where the stables were I did not know, but R—— offered his services as pilot, and we started out. Conditions seemed favorable. The day was fine. There were no wagons or drays to avoid. The streets were practically deserted. Everything went smoothly until we were about to cross Fifth Avenue, when a trotting horse, which two young men were speeding up the avenue, caught sight of the buffalo crossing the street ahead of her. There was a dash toward the lamp post, a wrecked road wagon, and a badly frightened horse flying up the avenue at a more than two-forty gait. "Don't stop! Don't look around! Hurry up!" called R___. "Turn down this side street, and let's push along as fast as possible." Push on we did until we had the buffalo safely locked up in a roomy stall with plenty of water and fodder. The next morning we scanned the daily papers carefully and felt relieved when no mention of the accident we had witnessed was to be found.

I called on the president and directors of the Crystal Palace to notify them of my arrival and to claim the space set aside for the Minnesota exhibit, including accommodation for a live buffalo. "A live buffalo!" exclaimed President Sedgwick in astonishment. "A live buffalo from the great plains of the West," he called out; "the latest arrival!" His outcry brought in several of the directors who were much impressed with the history of the exhibit. They all agreed that it would be of great interest to foreign visitors, but said that as yet no provision had been made for exhibiting live animals of any kind. They readily accepted my invitation to pay a visit to the stables to see the bison, and made arrangements to meet soon and decide what could be done about him. In the meantime I visited the Palace and attended to the placing of my exhibit in the space assigned me, which was somewhat larger than I could fill satisfactorily with the things I had on hand, unless the directors fixed a pen for the bison, a thing which I thought rather improbable. I arranged as attractively as possible the birchbark canoe and other Indian curios, the furs, my small stock of farm products, and a number of interesting photographs of Fort Snelling, the Falls of St. Anthony, and views of dog trains and Red River carts taken by Joel E. Whitney, St. Paul's first photographer which were adjudged superior to most of the photographic work exhibited. Finding that I still had considerable space at my command, I presented my letter from Mr. Sibley to Ramsay Crooks, who allowed me to select furs to any amount from the finest skins on the continent. I had noted the entire absence of any exhibit of agricultural products at the fair, so I called at Grant Thorburn's seed store and purchased seeds in quantities sufficient to supplement my rather meagre specimens from Minnesota. These seeds would also serve as standards by which to compare the grains grown on the new and fertile soil of Minnesota and which carried labels giving the name of the grower and the locality.

I had been an occasional correspondent for the *New York Tribune* for a few years, and I knew well the favorable reputation which Mr. Greeley held among the farmers of the country. Accordingly, I took him to see my Minnesota exhibit and especially invited a comparison of Minnesota grains with the best seed offered for sale by Grant Thorburn, then the leading seed man of the United States. I called his attention also to the fact that no other state or territory had an exhibit of agricultural products at the fair except Minnesota Territory, which he had once derided as a barren and inhospitable region, unsuitable for farming, fit only for logging operations. Mr. Greeley was completely surprised, and wrote a long editorial commenting on the evidences of fertility and adaptability of the soil of Minnesota for farming purposes as shown by the exhibit, and scoring the management for not securing from other states appropriate displays of their agricultural products. This notice in the *Tribune* started a tide of immigration to Minnesota which has continued in a steady stream ever since that day.

But to return to our bison. At the time appointed Mr. Sedgwick and a number of the directors of the fair — well-dressed, well-fed, jolly-countenanced men — met me at Bull's Head stables, where the buffalo was confined in a box stall, the door of which was hung on grooved wheels running on a rail at the top. As we were gathered about the stall, the hostler with sudden violence shoved the door back. The buffalo, who was lying down, probably asleep, sprang upon his feet, lowered his head as if about to charge, and uttered a little bellow, which sent the aldermanic crowd scattering in all directions. "Don't be skeered, gents," said the hostler; "he is perfectly harmless. He's probably more afraid than you 'uns is." But no explanations or assurances were of any avail. The hoped-for opportunity of unloading the buffalo on the Crystal Palace Company vanished with that scare. The directors had been obliged to hustle, to exert themselves. violently immediately after lunch, and there would be tailors' bills to pay. They had seen enough of the buffalo. He was *persona non grata* to them. I wrote to Cunradie an account of our safe arrival in New York; told him that the buffalo was eating his head off at Bull's Head stables, and that he must send me money with which to pay his board.

The opening exercises of the fair at the Crystal Palace were inaugurated by a speech by President Pierce. A great dinner was given at the Metropolitan Hotel, at which was served a portion of the new cereal from Minnesota, manomin or wild rice, a source of food supply for thousands of people and destined to be an important agricultural product because of its ability to grow in places where no other vegetation flourishes, as in water-covered swamps and along the margins of lakes.

The fair was progressing, and so were the expense bills, payable weekly, at Bull's Head stables. . . .

My good friend R—— came to the rescue. Among the side shows encamped round about the Palace was one containing a cinnamon bear, a moose, and a horned frog or two. R—— persuaded the owner that it would be to his advantage to increase his stock, and sold him the buffalo bull for three hundred dollars, to be paid in weekly installments at R——'s place of business. I took the first train out of New York for home. When R—— went to inquire why the first payment on the contract was not forthcoming, he found that the showman had departed for parts unknown, neglecting to leave any address. Long afterwards R—— wrote me that he had seen in a Maine newspaper an account of a man in that state of ice and pine lumber exhibiting a young buffalo bull, and he inquired if I had interest enough to look into the matter and, if possible, to identify the animal.

Some years after the fair I was sitting in the lobby of the Astor House, when suddenly there came up the steps a rush of arrivals from an Aspinwall steamer. Amid the hailing and handshaking and inquiries about friends in California, suddenly some one rushed up and shook a bronzed, cowboy-looking fellow by the hand, slapping him with friendly warmth on the shoulder. The rturned Californian cried out: "Don't, Jim, don't you know that's my broken shoulder, the one that was all smashed up three years ago at fair time. I'd just like to come across the son-of-a-gun that led that beast across the avenue as I was speeding my mare that day. I'll be darned if I wouldn't give him something to remember me by." As I felt no desire for an introduction to any member of the rough-looking party and especially to the excitable individual who seemed to nourish an unforgiving recollection of Cunradie's bison, I passed quietly down the steps and wandered thoughtfully up Broadway, gratified to know that the young man had suffered only a broken shoulder and two or three months under the surgeon's care. He might have been the principal in a funeral procession.

Having expended the three hundred dollars public money, and more of my own than was pleasant, I hastened to Mt. Vernon, Ohio, took my wife and baby, and returned to Minnesota by the quickest route, which was by rail to Chicago, then to Galena, and thence by boat to St. Paul, where, having reported to the new governor, Willis A. Gorman, I closed my commissionership.

The movement of immigration, begun in 1854 as a result of the exhibition of Minnesota products and of the editorial approval of Horace Greeley, has continued until the present day. A very large proportion of the immigrants were from the northern states. They were men and women educated in the common and high school, speaking our language, familiar with our forms of government, exemplary in their morals, with sound minds in sound bodies. Such were the people who laid the foundations of the state of Minnesota upon the basis of freedom of political and religious belief, freedom of opinion and action.

VII

Indian Trouble in St. Paul

Soon after the ratification of the treaty by which the lands of the Sioux Indians on the west side of the river were in possession of the United States, and were consequently open to settlement by citizens, a scramble began for preëmption and homestead claims. The demand for lumber for claim shanties in and around St. Paul, exceeded the production of the one little sawmill, and people stood waiting at the end of the mill for the board as it came from the saw. Having occasion to use some lumber for a claim of what is now a part of West St. Paul, I went early in the morning, the 29*th* of April, A.D. 1853, to the little mill, which stood three or four hundred yards east of where now stands the Union Depot, to secure some boards for my claim shanty. This sawmill, had been built by order of the American Fur Company, and was in charge of Mr. Charles Oakes of the firm of Borup and Oakes. The mill hands had not yet come to work, and the watchman informed me that Mr. Oakes was at the Santominie House, a new, large, three-story hotel that had been built for Mr. N. W. Kittson, on his addition to St. Paul, which had been platted, and was about to be put on the market. This house stood upon a bench of land across the swamp from the sawmill. Some slabs had been laid across the worst places in the swamp, and, by springing from one tussock to another, I crossed without getting deeply in the mud. I found Mr. Oakes in the large room of the house fronting the river, in which was a carpenter's bench, and a great many shavings, which had been used apparently for bedding by sixteen Chippewa Indians, whose blankets and other belongings were lying around. They were listening to Mr. Oakes, who was talking very earnestly with them, trying to persuade them to return home without molesting the Sioux of Little Crow's village, whose scalps they had come to obtain. As Mr. Oakes had married in their tribe, they expected his help. Little Crow's village was only six miles down the river, on the west side, and they were anxious to acquaint themselves with its exact location.

I finally had an opportunity to talk with Mr. Oakes, who gladly promised to let me have the lumber to get rid of me, and, as I started to go out the door, I saw some of the Indians looking excitedly down the river, and, turning my eyes in the same direction, I saw a canoe with three Sioux Indians coming around the point. They were paddling rapidly close to the bank on the west side, a man and two women, the man steering, and the women sending the canoe along rapidly. I started at a fast walk up the path, through the brush leading to a log bridge which had been built across the deep ravine on Jackson Street, in front of Lot Moffat's "castle" — so called. This ravine was thirty or more feet deep, with very steep sides, covered with a thick growth of brush. The bushes along the path which I was following were mostly higher than my head, but there were places where, looking through, I could see the canoe of the Sioux making good progress to the landing at the foot of Jackson Street. Hearing some moccasined footfalls behind me I turned, and saw the Chippewas following close at my heels, crouched down, so as not to be seen, with their guns en trail. As I kept on going westward in the path they were not willing to follow further — not knowing of the ravine, or the bridge — they feared the path led away from their game, and, dropping off their blankets, and other impedimenta, they started south, through the brush, direct to where they expected the three Sioux would land. This move saved the lives of two of the Sioux, as they had time to get inside the door of Forbes' store before the Chippewas, who met with unexpected difficulties climbing down and up the sides of the difficult ravine, came out on Third Street, and fired a volley — uttering their war whoop — at the Indians entering the store. Old "Wooden-legged Jim" and his sister "Betts" had passed through the door, and the younger sister was entering as they fired. A ball went through her body. The others were not injured. It was said that old Jim dropped behind a post in the store, and opend fire on the Chippewas with his gun. This I do not believe, as I saw no evidence of firing from the store, and I was not a hundred feet distant, and saw and heard it all.

A recent excavation in grading Third Street had left the store eight or ten feet above the street, and a broad flight of steps led up to the store-front from the street. On the opposite side the cut was a little higher, and was nearly perpendicular. Down this face the Indians scrambled, and ran across the street and up the steps. Meanwhile there was some activity inside the store. The demoniac yelling of the savages, and the firing of sixteen balls into the store, in which were, at the time, Forbes, Theodore Borup, David Oakes, and Sweet, who had married a Chippewa woman, and who was a relative of the Borup and Oakes boys. These three rushed out to thrust the Indians back, while Forbes barred the door behind them, the boys haranguing the Chippewas all the time, as they pushed them down the steps, telling them that the Governor would send soldiers from Fort Snelling to punish them for firing into a white man's store. Seeing that they could not get scalps they finally departed, and, having obtained some food supplies from their relatives, were hurried, disappointed, out of town.

As soon as Governor Ramsey heard of the outrage, he ordered out the militia, and sent a requisition to the Fort for a squadron of cavalry to be sent in pursuit of the marauders, to drive them back to the St. Croix, where they came from. Captain Simpson, a regular army officer of the engineer department, who was in charge of the construction of military roads in the Territory, was put in command of the militia, who were ordered to report on horseback at the corner of Third and Jackson Streets, as soon as possible. Every horse in town was put in requisition, private as well as livery stable horses, and all told, they did not exceed twenty, I think. Saddles were scarce. Guns were of all kinds, but mostly rifles; but we started out — such a mob as we were — about eleven o'clock, to follow the trial of the sixteen Chippewa Indians, eager for a frolic — for I think not one of us expected to find the Indians.

There was no difficulty in following the trail as far as a large lake, and here we lost it; they had evidently taken to the water, but where they had gone — whether up or down the lake — no one could tell. Captain Simpson ordered an inspection of arms, and it was found that, either through ignorance or carelessness, some of the militia had loaded their rifles with the ball down first. At the distance of fifty paces, firing at a target placed on a large tree, some missed the tree. While thus engaged two horsemen were seen approaching through the woods, their persons and horses encumbered with various bundles and bags, and, as they came nearer, we discovered that they were commissaries of subsistence, Governor Ramsey and Mr. Oakes, loaded with packages of crackers, cheese, dried venison, and the like. The two demijohns hung on either side to the cantle of the Governor's saddle gave evidence of the thoughtfulness of His Excellency lest some one should get hurt, or snake bitten.

The commissary stores, solid and liquid, soon vanished, and with hunger unappeased, the volunteers clamored for more. Someone noticed that toward the southeast, an occasional tapping was heard, not unlike the tapping of the large redheaded woodpecker, but sometimes louder. A mounted scout was sent to investigate, and returned with the information that the noise was from the blows of a hammer; that Bill Branch had some carpenters at work building a house for De Montreville, a St. Louis dentist, who proposed to spend his summer on the shore of the lake. We learned further that by riding some miles to the southeast we could find Jack Morgan's halfway house and get something to eat. Branch had seen no Indians, nor any indications of Indians.

We rode through the woods to Morgan's, and ordered some dinner. They said they were not prepared to feed so many people on such short notice, but would cook what there was in the house, which they did, and we had a small ration each. While we were at dinner Lieutenant McGruder came with the detachment sent by the commandant of the fort, and reported to the governor for orders. He was directed to proceed toward the Indian country on the St. Croix, and if he saw any party of Indians, to drive them home. . . .

Having eaten all that could be obtained at Morgan's, the militia returned to St. Paul, and dispersed. Not having been formally mustered into service, we made no claim for pay or land warrants, nor so far as I have heard, has anyone obtained a pension on account of the brief expedition against the audacious, scalp-hunting Chippewas, who killed a woman in the street in St. Paul, in April, A.D. 1853.

VIII

Railroads and Land

The rapid settlement of the lower part of the state, and the large increase in the steamboat business, excited the greed of speculators in railroad enterprises, and delegations of self-represented capitalists made friends and partners of St. Paul men. They obtained charters for railroads from St. Paul to Stillwater, to Breckenridge on the Red River, and to Prairie Du Chien — kite-flying projects all, but there was the firm conviction that they must be built sometime — and they have been.

Those who were most active in railroad matters were Milwaukee people who had friends in the legislature. There was, of course, opposition, and the governor was the leader, backed by others who were believed to have a scheme for the removal of the capital to a new town in which they had title. They wanted to defeat any charter for a company that would build a railroad to St. Paul. The opposition well knew that popular feeling was against them, and did not wish openly to antagonize the friends of the charter, but managed by various delays to put off the final vote in council until the last day of the session.

I had a preëmption matter to defend at Kaposia, and there I met a friend of mine who was of the same party, politically, as the governor. Talking with him I told him we had enough votes in the council to pass the bill, and that it would be done. "Very well," he said, "the friends of the bill may pass it, but it will never become a law. The Governor will veto it."

"No," I said, "he will never do that. He proclaims his love for the people, and for majority rule on all occasions — he won't". But I felt sure that he had the promise of a veto from the governor himself. I was earnestly interested in the passage of the charter.

As soon as my client's business permitted I hastened to St. Paul, and finding a friend who was equally interested, I told him what we might expect from the action of the governor. "If he does that," he said, "we are beaten, for it is near the last hours of the session, and we have not votes now to pass it over his veto." But I said: "Don't give up yet. I think we can get up a demonstration of the people. Let us try the effect of petitions on him. Divide up the town into districts. I will take one section — Masterton can take another — and wake up people to sign. Others can take other parts of the town and fire the petitions at him as fast as possible. Meanwhile you see Charlie Bazille, and rouse the French habitants."

It was the last night of the session. Our friends in the legislature prevented adjournment. Many of the citizens we found asleep, but they awoke and willingly consented to sign the petition. When I had a goodly number of names on the one I was circulating, I hastened to present it, saying: "Governor, I have the honor to present to your Excellency a petition of the people."

"Petition — petition — " he exclaimed, "I don't want to receive any petitions here — at this time of night!"

"It may be a little late, Governor, but you surely will not refuse the right of petition, or neglect to read the prayer of the petitioners, whenever they ask to be heard; in a democratic government this right can not be questioned."

Soon after Masterton came in with his, then another and another, until the Governor excitedly sprang from his chair, and emphatically declared: "I won't receive another one!"

Word was passed out to Bazille, and soon shouts of execration filled the air from the crowd that was holding an indignation meeting outside the capitol building. The natural vivacity of the French had been stimulated by whiskey, and the crowd was increasing in numbers and noisy demonstration every moment. "Get a rope and hang that ——— to an oak" was heard. Someone took the secretary of the Territory out into the noisy, threatening crowd, and the secretary went in to the governor and told him what he had seen and heard. The governor sent a messenger to the president of the council, asking him to adjourn the council, as it was after twelve o'clock. The president of the council refused to adjourn until the business was finished. The governor then sent up the bill signed "under protest."

The president of the council was a warm opponent of the bill, and when he received it he opened it with infinite disgust on his expressive face. "Signed," he exclaimed, *"signed under protest!* This Council may now be properly adjourned." The mob outside was duly informed, and they kept up their celebration until morning. The railroad bill was a law, but it proved to be hasty and unwise legislation, afterward much regretted. . . .

Sometime during the summer of 1855 A.D. a friend of mine from Ohio came to St. Paul, where he saw by a notice in a newspaper that the government surveyors had discovered a trout stream a few miles south of Oliver's Grove (afterward Hastings). He and I, wanting some fishing, took a livery team and drove to the landing. Here we crossed the Mississippi in a little flat boat. The ferryman said he had heard the surveyors talk about that trout stream, and that by following the survey stakes we could not miss it. He also wanted to know more about it, and would go with us as a guide. It was late in the day, and he led off at a rapid walk. After crossing the Vermillion River, or creek, he soon found the first survey stake, and we started south on the marked line across a beautiful prairie. The buggy was a narrow seated vehicle, hardly wide enough for two. The ferryman was very large and heavy, and could not be induced to take the place of one of us, and ride until rested. He had become heated by the time we reached the big spring from which the trout brook flowed, and putting his head down to the water, he filled himself with the cool, refreshing liquid. Soon after he was doubled up with colic and chills. We rubbed him and worked with him the entire night, giving him all the whiskey we had, until daylight enabled us to trace the track we had made. We returned to Bailey's trading post at the landing, where, with plenty of whiskey, he got permanent relief.

As we forded the Vermillion on our return trip, a man accosted me whom I recognized as a client of mine, named Graham, a millwright, for whom I had acted in a law suit in St. Paul. He wished to see me on some business, and followed us down to Bailey's, and explained the situation. He had made claim to eighty acres of land embracing a part of the falls of the Vermillion, and had built a board shanty, and was living there with his wife and children. Some St. Paul speculators had sent a man named Jim Main to hold the falls of the Vermillion. This man had no house and no family, only a brush shelter under which he slept, with a shotgun beside him. He ordered Graham to get off. He was holding the claim for others — whose names he gave. These claims were both made before the survey lines were established. After the survey it was evident that Graham and Main were both on the same quarter section, Graham being an actual settler, with his family on the land, and Main an employee of others. I advised Graham that he was in right of possession; that he should claim the full quarter section, and, if Main was objectionable, drive him off.

Later — at the proper time — I appeared with Graham and his witnesses, at the land office at Red Wing, to prove his settlement and his right to enter the land. On my demand for a hearing I was informed that there was a contest noted in the case, and it would be heard two weeks from date. Having been given the name of the attorney for the contestants, I went to his office, when the time for the hearing came, and offered him a seat in my sleigh, as it was lonely riding alone, and the ice in the river was getting unsafe. He said he knew the ice was bad. He had heard that a man with a team had broken through near Red Rock, and he tried to persuade me to postpone the trip, but I had promised my client to meet him at Hastings, and I said I would go that far if no farther.

He said he would not go, for all the land in Minnesota, at the risk of his life, but if I was foolish enough to go, would I take a carpetsack Phelps had left when he was last up — it had not much in it — maybe a soiled shirt or two. "Yes," I said, "but I may send it down from Hastings. Nothing valuable in it, I suppose?" "No," he answered, "send it from Hastings if you wish to."

While driving down, with the carpetbag for company, it occurred to me that I had not heard of Phelps being in St. Paul lately, and that such an old carpetbag seemed hardly suitable for Phelps to carry, and possibly it might have an affidavit in it for a continuance in the Graham case; and, as I thought it over, I became pretty sure that I was carrying a club for my injury. At Hastings I found Mr. Bailey, and explained the situation to him, and asked him, as he was going home after a few days, and had to pass through Red Wing, to take charge of the carpetbag, and deliver it. He loved a joke, and gladly consented, and I put it into his hands for delivery.

I took Graham and his two witnesses in my sleigh, and went to Red Wing, proved up my case, and demanded the certificate. The officers hesitated, and finally declined to give the certificate. They said they were sure a contest was intended in this case. They were new to the business, but they would ask the opinion of Doctor Hoyt, an experienced officer at Hudson, Wisconsin. If he advised it, they would issue the certificate. They would write a letter to Hoyt, and I might deliver it and bring the answer. This was evidently a ruse to gain time to send to St. Paul to notify the attorney of our opponents.

I told Graham I thought we could checkmate the move by getting the letter to Doctor Hoyt at Hudson and an answer back before they could get notice to the parties adverse in St. Paul. I took him and his two witnesses in my sleigh and drove at a lively gait to Hastings, leaving one of the witnesses concealed at the crossing of the river at Point Douglas, where the Hastings road diverged from the St. Paul road, to note if any messenger was sent from Red Wing to St. Paul. About dark he came and reported that Day, of Red Wing, had passed up toward St. Paul in a hurry. I got a fresh team, and with Graham, started at about eight o'clock over the bluffs for Hudson, twenty or more miles away. We had never been there, but had the general direction. There was snow on the ground — more than plenty in some of the drifts we encountered. There was no road until we found the trail from Stillwater to Hudson, which we then followed across Lake St. Croix, and, by disturbing some sleepers, found the house of the land officer, Doctor Hoyt, at two o'clock in the morning. I explained the necessity which compelled this early visit, delivered the letter, and listened with approval to the old Doctor's emphatic English and Latin denunciation of the two land speculators, who had caused him no end of trouble, and of the land officers at Red Wing, who were being decoyed by them. He wrote a fiery letter to Phelps and Graham, and advised us that we would have no difficulty in getting our certificate, and told us to be very careful of the ice on the lake.

We were back at Hastings to breakfast, and soon on our way to Red Wing, where we delivered Doctor Hoyt's letter, and watched the countenances of the officers change as they read his denunciations. The certificate was issued, and I sent it by the next mail to Washington, to our delegate, the Honorable Henry M. Rice, and requested him to see that the patent was put through the land office. I soon had the pleasure of delivering to Graham the title to his land. He was much pleased, and said to me: "I started to get eighty acres, and you have got one hundred and sixty for me. You have paid all the expenses, and paid for the land entry. I have nothing to pay back that money with, nor to pay you for your services. I am a millwright, and can build a little mill on this power, if you will put up money for the materials, and it will make money from the start, for settlers coming in on these fertile lands must raise grain, and must bring it to the mill to be ground. Now will you take a deed of half interest in the quarter section, and call it even?"

To this I assented, and thus became interested in Vermillion Falls. Graham soon prepared the plans for a mill, and commenced the erection of a building forty by sixty feet, with two stories and an attic, and a basement in which was the wheelpit, using a head of water eighteen feet. He selected an oak tree about sixteen inches in diameter, and rounded the bottom to fit a cast iron cup; on the top was the runner, half of a pair of French burr stones four and a half feet in diameter. At the bottom of this shaft a flutter-wheel was built, and the water led down to it by a strong box near the top of the shaft. A wooden friction wheel was built which ran the smut mills, bolting chest, and whatever else required motion from the belts.

The mill did good work, and there was plenty of work for it to do, as soon as finished sufficiently to grind anything. The first merchantable flour made in Minnesota was made here. The mill was improved and enlarged constantly, but never finished. Graham thought he saw a good chance to build a mill on the Cannon River, and wanted to sell. I bought his interest and, about the same time, bought a one fourth interest in the town site of Hastings. This town site claim was made by Alexis Bailley, and Henry G. Bailley, who took in, as partners, J. B. Faribault, Bailley's father-in-law, and Henry Hastings Sibley, each having one fourth interest. A portion of the site claimed had been roughly surveyed, and staked out in town lots. Faribault and his son-in-law were not in harmony, and Sibley sold to me for him his one-fourth interest, one-half of which I afterward sold to W. K. Rogers. My interests were now more in Hastings than in St. Paul, and I sold my book business, and my house and lot at the corner of Third and Wabasha Streets, also my West St. Paul property, and moved my family to Hastings, and took charge of the town site and the milling business. I built a comfortable dwelling house near the mill. I put in an overshot wheel and doubled the capacity of the mill, which was then taxed to the limit, and would need further enlargements.

When moving from St. Paul I chartered a small steamer to transport my household goods and other belongings, among which, I remember, were two dogs: one of them was a pointer puppy Sibley had given me a few weeks before, that grew up to make a famous hunting dog. During the night preceeding the day we moved from St. Paul this recently weaned pup, named Bruno, acquired a friend, whom he brought with him, when I called him from the woodshed to his breakfast, a strong, full grown mastiff, one of whose eyes had been destroyed in a recent fight. I was about to drive him away when Bruno looked up at me, with a beseeching face, asking me to let the mastiff share his breakfast, and the stray mastiff looked so dignified and humble that I fed both. I did not expect to see the tramp dog again, but when, later in the day, our things were being taken on the steamboat, Bruno and his friend came on board without an invitation, and both dogs lived and died in my service — faithful dogs, and firm friends to the last. The pointer would sometimes take the mastiff out on the praire, and station him on a rise of ground, and then circle round and point prairie chickens, and, after a little waiting, rush in and put them to flight. But the mastiff could not be coaxed to go hunting if the children were about the yard. And when the baby was taken to ride by the nurse in his little carriage the mastiff was always on guard, and would keep all animals at a respectable distance; and tramps were recognized as persons not to be admitted to the house or yard.

IX

Preparations for War

Immigrants were thronging into Minnesota from the eastern states and from Europe, and the helping of incoming settlers to acquire their preëmption claims, and buying and selling of real estate, and the milling business, which was increasing daily — customers coming from as far south as the Iowa line to have their grain ground — made full and profitable employment for my time, up to the period of the political disturbance in the slave-holding states. The disappointment and turbulence of the people of the South after the election of Lincoln to the presidency made it evident to me that a war between the states was certain to occur.

Having traveled extensively through the South and being thus familiar with the people and their feelings and their ways, I was astonished to hear Mr. Seward (afterward President Lincoln's Secretary of State) in a public speech in St. Paul, say that there was no danger of any serious trouble with the South. Knowing his error, and that such erroneous opinion expressed by one so prominent in public life could only lessen the chances of averting war, I consulted with a friend, a graduate of West Point who had seen honorable service in the war with Mexico, and asked him how best I could serve the country in the impending struggle. He agreed with me in believing war between the North and South inevitable, and said: "War is business, and the best business capacity, backed by the longest purse, is sure to win. The South will be conquered, her slaves freed, her people impoverished. You say you know nothing of military matters, but desire to take up that part of the business you can most readily acquire, and where your services will be most effective. I think you are best fitted by natural and acquired qualifications for service in the quarter-master's department. This is a very important department of army service. An inefficient quartermaster department will render use-less the best military organization, commanded by the best officers. It is through this bureau that all army supplies of whatever kind are obtained, transported, issued to troops, accounted for, and returns made to the Treasury Department of the general govern-ment. The difficult and intricate duties of the department require men of wide range of knowledge and experience; of willing hearts, and untiring zeal. No army can be efficient without the prompt exercise of their duties. At the same time there is more work than in any other branch of the service, and less chance for advancement in rank and pay. The officers who direct or lead troops in battle, are — if they come out alive — those whom the people delight to honor. But the man whose business skill, energy and fertility of resource makes possible the marching and fighting of an army, rarely gains fame beyond the commander, or the troops with whom he serves. I, having been educated at West Point, will, of course, tender my services, and, from my experience, will expect to com-mand a brigade. And if you should apply for and obtain an ap-pointment as captain and assistant quartermaster, I wish you would ask to be assigned to my command. You know I have been in that department, and can help you to get a start. I will be at the front somewhere, and I advise you to try and keep with the troops in active work." Having determined to follow my friend's advice, I commenced at once to close up my business affairs, and in the winter of 1861 and '62, left Minnesota for Washington to seek the appointment of captain and assistant quartermaster. I had previously sold to Harrison Brothers ten acres and the mill, and conveyed by proper legal deeds to my wife the remainder of the hundred and sixty acres of the mill property, and had con-tracted for the erection of a house for her.

I stopped over in Ohio and obtained letters of introduction from several friends, who were also friends of Secretary Stanton, and one in particular from a distant cousin, John Miner, who, in youthful days, had been Stanton's most intimate friend. Armed with these I went to Washington, confident of success, as our con-gressional delegation was also friendly. Having the introductory note and endorsement of Senator Rice, I arrayed my papers in lawyer-like shape, and indexed on the outside, "Application of

Wm. G. Le Duc for appointment as Captain and Assistant Quartermaster, and assignment to Dana's Brigade, supported by senators and representatives from Minnesota, and by letters from John Miner of Cincinnati, R. C. Hurd, and Henry B. Curtis, of Mt. Vernon, Ohio." I sought an interview with the Secretary, who had a high desk outside the door of his room in the War Department beside which he stood receiving people who had business with the Department, a long line of whom extended down the hall. I took my place in the line, and had ample opportunity to observe, as the procession of men approached the desk, one at a time, how each, being given a hearing, was dismissed in a few words. When my turn came he was standing behind the desk, leaning one tired arm on it. Reading the introduction from Senator Rice, and from John Miner, and looking me in the face, he said, in a weary voice, "Where do you live?"

I answered, "Hastings, Minnesota."

He made a memorandum, and said: "Your commission will be issued, and sent to Minnesota."

I reported to Senator Rice, and he said he would look after it, and I returned home to make arrangements to take my wife and children to Ohio, after storing our household goods in a carriage-house and barn I had built.

In due time the commission came, and I was required to give bonds, in a large sum, for the faithful performance of my duty. Mr. Charles Oakes and Captain Davidson were my bondsmen. I took my wife and children to Mt. Vernon, Ohio, and left them with her mother. Here I found my wife's brother, Charles Bronson, who had tried to get into the military service as an enlisted soldier, but was not physically competent, and was much disappointed. I offered him a clerkship, which he gladly accepted, and we reported at Washington, and I was assigned to the Third Brigade, Third Division, Second Corps, Army of the Potomac, then on the Peninsula under command of General McClellan. I was furnished transportation on one of the government steamers running from Baltimore to Fortress Monroe, the Potomac River being at that time blockaded by the rebels.

We arrived at the fortress at ten o'clock, Monday, the 19*th* of May, A.D. 1862, and, finding a boat ready to leave for the front, took passage thereon, and arrived at White House Landing, Pamunky River, at five o'clock P.M. Steamers and sailing vessels of all sorts filled the stream, and crowded the landing. A large force of men were engaged in unloading stores, guns, ammunition, and every conceivable munition of war. We stepped from the deck of the steamer to the deck of Quartermaster Wagner's wharf and storage barge; from the steady going ways of civil life into the very vortex of the cyclone of army life; and for three and a half years I was one of the atoms "in God's great storm that roared through the angry skies."

An officer seated at a table with a pencil and memorandum book before him, and several clerks near at hand, all busy, looked up as we entered his office, with a tired, appealing look, which I soon interpreted to mean 'Please don't take any more time to state your business than is necessary'. He said: "I am Captain Wagner, in charge here. Can I do anything for you?"

"I do not know, sir. I am Captain Le Duc, Assistant Quartermaster, recently appointed, and assigned to Dana's Brigade, Sedgewick's Division, Sumner's Corps."

"I am glad to see you and make your acquaintance," he answered, "and wish you had been assigned here, where we need more help. Your corps is advancing today, and a part of Dana's Brigade is guarding the stores and landing. General Dana will be along tomorrow, and you will easily find your command — it is too late today. Take a bunk" (two pairs of army blankets on some board slats) "on this barge for tonight, and start fair in the morning. Meanwhile you will want horses, and an outfit of desks and stationery, which you can select, and receipt for."

Having given orders . . . he turned to the increasing crowd around his table, and took up the eternal burden of a quartermaster's duties, with commendable patience. I selected two horses of medium size, apparently the best in the corral, but both unfit for the saddle, and which were exchanged by wagonmaster Felch, of Dana's brigade, for better ones, one of which I kept with me during the entire period of my service in the Army of the Potomac and of the Cumberland, and which I left in charge of my orderly, when I had leave of absence, in Atlanta. The army moved before my return, the orderly was killed, and the horse captured in South Carolina. He was black as a raven, with small ears set on a handsome head, with blazing eyes, when excited, broad nostrils, thin neck, round body, flat legs — a thoroughbred that would not work in harness, nor submit, without the protest of bucking, to be ridden by anyone he did not like. We made friends from the start, and a better horse for army service it would be hard to find. His appetite and digestion were good; he would forage whenever and wherever there was opportunity, and appropriate either Union or Rebel grain or hay, if within his reach. His intelligence and ingenuity were remarkable, and, night or day, he was sure-footed as a mule, and could go with the best, and endure to the last. A saddle horse rarely equalled was Black Jim. . . .

In the morning I found that Dana's Brigade had gone forward to Cumberland, to which place I rode and reported to General Dana for assignment to duty, the 20th of May, 1862. On the 21st I was announced in orders as the Quartermaster of the Brigade, and, taking command of the transportation and ammunition trains, I moved them eight and a half miles to a camp near the Richmond and West Point railroad. The officer whom I relieved was a lieutenant of the line, detailed for this duty for a short time, who knew little and cared less for the business connected with it. The regimental quartermasters were intelligent and willing, and, by their assistance, my clerk and I soon became familiar with the various forms of account, and methods of making requisitions and obtaining supplies, and we thus commenced the endless duties of this department serving with troops in the field in active warfare.

On the 22nd of May, late in the afternoon, I started, with all available teams, to bring supplies from the White House depot. The night was dark, the road unknown to me, and so muddy that, on level ground, the horses were splashing through a bed of thin mortar, and the wagons would sometimes drop to the axle in mud holes. Lieutenant Garland, a Regimental Quartermaster, whom I had taken with me, had been over the road once, and, knowing the general direction, we rode ahead of the train to guide and direct. Knowing that we should turn to the left, and go eastward where we came to the Bottom Bridge Road, we were alert and anxious, lest, in the darkness, we should pass the junction, and run into the lines of the enemy. This anxiety became intense as we entered a wood, heard the tramp of marching men, and felt their presence, for we could not see them. We halted, and at the same time were challenged with: "Who goes there?"

Garland answered, "Friends — Brigade Train — Sumner's Corps — going to White House for supplies. Who are you?"

"Kearney's Division, marching to the front by way of Bottom's

Bridge. All right. Turn sharp to the left here, if you go to White House."

"All right," and we turned to the left, and soon met Kearney's trains, floundering through the mud, making such progress as was possible in the dense darkness. Several of the wagons were hopelessly fast, the teams taken off, and tethered in the woods. I remember one team stuck in mud and water halfway to the horses' bellies, and the driver asleep. We had to build a fire by the road side to enable us to see how to get by, and shortly after getting to dry ground we camped by a large spring and waited for daylight. In the morning I proceeded to the depot to draw supplies, instructed by Garland in the use of that all powerful paper, a requisition, properly signed and verified — the requisition of the commanding officer, backed by the receipt of the quartermaster, being a sufficient settlement of account with the depot officer. The officer receiving the property, or money, then becomes responsible, and either turns it over to other officers, on like vouchers, or if ammunition, or forage, expends it as such; if food, clothing, or garrison equipment, issues it to the troops, or wears it out in the service. This simple but thorough system of accountability suffices to transfer, expend, and accurately account for millions of dollars worth of property or money, without loss to the government.

On the 23*rd* I returned to the Brigade, and found it had moved forward to Savage's farm, and it was with difficulty that supplies could be brought to the troops in wagons, as they would frequently drop through the surface soil and rest on the axles. . . .

On the 24*th* we marched westward four or five miles, and camped on Tyler's farm, with the Chickahominy swampy bottom-lands in our front, General Sumner's Headquarters being in the Tyler house yard. There we remained undisturbed, and on the 26*th* were building the grapevine bridge. The Chickahominy Creek, at this place, is an insignificant stream, with only two to four feet of water and mud, twenty to thirty feet wide when all together, but divided into several channels, and running through a heavily wooded swamp, four or five hundred yards wide. When the stream rises a few feet above the ordinary summer level, this swamp is inundated, and the bottom lands, which intervene between the swamp and the higher lands, are little elevated at their margins from the swamp, and so a rise of a few feet of the river covers large areas. The rich and cultivated bottom lands are very soft, without corduroy or stone made roads, and are impracticable for artillery, or wagon transportation of the army.

On the 27*th* I took the cars at Dispatch Station, to go to White House to obtain and forward supplies over the railroad, which had been furnished with engine and cars from Washington. In passing at a short distance from the Chickahominy, I noticed a little sawmill, and, on a siding, two cars loaded with lumber, ready for shipping, which subsequently served a very important purpose. The depot quartermaster had compelled order out of the chaos existing previously, and my requisitions were promptly filled, and I returned by rail on the 28*th*, and found the troops had been ordered out, with three days' rations, to hasten the completion of the bridge, and cut a road through the bottoms to and from the grapevine bridge. May 30*th* I issued clothing and camp supplies to the troops, and sent teams to Despatch Station four miles distant for supplies. They were the entire day in going and returning, nearly all the time being expended in returning, loaded. The ground was so soft that loaded wagons would cut through the top soil, and have to be unloaded and dug or pried out.

Being short of forage, I seized nearly all that a farmer (Charles Baker) had, which was of little value, as it was corn blades, the only kind of coarse fodder the Virginia farmers save for their stock. A while after this I ascended rising ground three or more miles west from our camp, and the elevation was such that I could see far across the river, and could hear, indistinctly, musketry firing, and thought some skirmish was taking place, but as the firing increased in volume, and the smoke of the conflict rose above the tree tops, and the voice of the great guns began to emphasize the noise, I noticed that the white cloud was moving eastward; apparently our men were being driven. I then hastened back to camp, and found our corps moving across the grapevine bridge, marching light, with one day's rations. I hastened to join General Dana, before he got on the bridge, and he ordered me to return to camp, take charge of it, and await further orders.

X

The Chickahominy Campaign

About eleven o'clock that night orders were received from General Sumner directing the quartermasters of the corps to turn out with every available man in camp, camp guard and officers, servants — and all of the sick able to do anything — to help the artillery through the mud and across the Chickahominy. The swamp on the north side was about three quarters of a mile wide, and was full of artillery caissons and ammunition wagons, all trying to get to and on the crooked grapevine bridge, but prevented from moving by the leading teams being fast in some mud hole, or against stumps or trees. The horses were exhausted, and the men and officers discouraged.

Guns and caissons were down to the hub in many places. Getting them out — in darkness — and with a drizzling rain — seemed almost a hopeless task, but it must be done by or before daylight, as a severe fight had occurred, and would be renewed in the morning, and everything depended on getting the artillery over before the enemy could attack.

The corps quartermaster was reported sick or drunk; he did not make his appearance. All was in confusion when Captain Bachelder and I arrived at the end of the bridge. He said: "You take charge here, and I'll go to the other side, and help there." He went, and, as the bridge was so narrow, he could not return until all were over. I hitched my horse to a limb and getting into the water up to the knees or middle, called some men around me, and we lifted the wheels of the gun carriages and wagons out of ruts or around stumps, and, one by one, worried the teams to the bridge head.

In the woods it was impossible to see but for some candles which the artillerymen had fastened on stumps or trees, and which were mostly extinguished by the rain. I had noticed a fence of oak rails, as I rode by before dark, and, getting some of these, made torches, such as I had used when a boy in Ohio, hunting coons; and putting them in the hands of the sick or feeble we had the swamp pretty well illuminated, and the work went on all night, until every battery was put on the bridge except one — that of a regular officer, who would not risk his guns to cross that crooked bridge in the darkness, so he outspanned, and fed and rested until morning, and no doubt got over the bridge in time to do good service.

When this last battery had started over the bridge it was daylight, and I sat on a log, waiting for Captain Bachelder to return. Looking at the stream, I saw the middle full of drift, and that it was rising rapidly, and I stuck my knife in a log at the water's edge, and took out my watch, and, when Captain Bachelder returned noted the time, and the distance from the water to the bridge stringers, and called his attention to the short distance from the water to the bridge logs, and we rode back toward camp. As we passed by Corps Headquarters, I noticed some officers, one of whom I recognised as an old college acquaintance and, stopping my horse, called out: "Hello, Nels. Some of you people ought to know that the grapevine bridge is going out in two hours."

One of them said: "It can't be possible."

I replied: "It is not only possible, but it is certain to go if the river keeps on rising for two hours, and I regard that as a sure thing." I heard a stir in the tent in front of which we were stopping, and a head appeared in the opening, and a voice expressing the utmost concern asked: "How do you know that, sir?"

I replied: "I have been there all night, and I have timed the rise of the river, which is now nearly up to the stringers, and go it must, unless the stream stops rising, which is not probable."

"Can't you get some rocks, and pile on the timbers?"

"No, there are no rocks in this quicksand country; none large enough to throw at a bird — much less to weight down bridge timbers."

"Put on some logs."

"That would only make it worse, as it would offer greater resistance to the current."

"Tie the logs down with ropes."

"There is nothing to tie to but the stringers, and they would all

73

float off together. But why care for this wretched grapevine bridge?"

"Because it is the only communication with the army on the other side."

"What's to hinder using the railroad bridge, a quarter of a mile below? It is high above all water, and there's ample space between the trestle work for the water to pass. I passed it a few days ago, and had the curiosity to examine it, and found it to be in good condition for railroad trains, and consequently all that is necessary is to plank it. According to my rough measurement, counting my steps, it was thirteen hundred feet across the trestle work, and the steep embankment on the other side was seventeen hundred feet; and on the north side, three hundred feet. The approaches are probably practicable; on the north side certainly — and there are two cars of lumber standing on a side track at a little sawmill a mile or two down the track, which can be pushed down to the bridge; then it can be speedily planked."

"Can you plank that bridge?"

"Certainly — anybody can do it."

The General (for it was General McClellan whose head was talking out of the folds of the tent) said to one of his staff: "Issue an order to this officer to plank that bridge," hearing which I said: "I don't belong here. I am in Dana's Brigade that has gone across the river."

Bachelder, who was alongside of me, said: "Don't you know that is General McClellan?"

"Yes, of course I know him. He married in my country. I knew him there, but I did not come down here to be ordered about by everybody," and we rode on to our own tents, to get some breakfast, while Bachelder explained to me that McClellan, being commander-in-chief, could order Sumner, and he Sedgewick, and he Dana, and finally Dana could order me, but that it would be well to take the order from Headquarters direct.

I soon received the following order:

"Headquarters Army, Potomac, June 1st, A. D. 1862. General McClellan directs that Captain W. G. Le Duc shall plank the railroad bridge across the Chickahominy River, and that all officers in command of guards, etc., of our army give him all the assistance he may require for that purpose; should the descent from the opposite side not be practicable, he will not be required to do this duty after making a reconnaissance. Signed A. W. Putnam, Captain A. Q. M. Second Corps."

I said, "To do this work I must have tools — saws, hammers or hatchets, and nails." There were no hammers nor hatchets nor nails, and but three saws, new, and not set or filed, and consequently of no use. There was a box of axes, but no helves, and a keg of spikes. One of my own men took the axes in hand, and made some sort of handles out of what he could pick up, and with these to use, in place of saws and hammers, I took up the job of planking the bridge. The sawmill was some miles away. I sent some men to shove the cars holding lumber down or up to the bridge, (whether the grade was up or down I do not know), but it took all day to get the cars to the bridgehead, and there were then only a few hours of daylight left. Meanwhile, as I had all the men that could be employed on the work, the time spent waiting for the lumber was profitably employed in making the approaches practicable. The planking was done in three and a half hours when we got at it, and the bridge was immediately brought into use by the passage of an ambulance train and of cavalry and infantry.

I telegraphed to White House to have some planks and tools sent up to make the bridge passable for artillery and loaded wagons, and reported the facts to General McClellan, who thought I should go myself to White House and personally see that there was no delay possible in getting the necessary planks and carpenters to make the bridge passable for all arms. This I did, and returned with a train of lumber and workmen with tools, at three o'clock in the morning of the third day of June. After setting the men at work, I returned to brigade headquarters to get some rest and sleep, and did not awaken until the morning of the fourth, and found the earth flooded by a tremendous rain, which entirely covered the bottoms of the Chickahominy, and rendered all other bridges useless except my railroad bridge which was fifteen feet above high water, and safe. Men were sent to the grapevine bridge, and to Bottoms Bridge, to try and secure the logs and hold them ready for use when the water receded.

On the fifth of June, being at Dispatch Station, near the bridge, I went down to examine it, and found that the rapid current had commenced to undermine the embankment on the northern side of the stream, and the end timbers had settled some eight inches. I took the responsibility of acting under my former orders, and had men detailed from the station guard, with axes, and made a coffer dam, with boards and slabs around the end of the embankment, keyed up the middle of the bridge, which had settled out of line, and fixed up the end timbers, so as to make it safe for the passage of engines and trains. Passing from the bridge toward Dispatch Station, I saw that the embankment which filled in a deep ravine over a circular brick culvert of about eight feet radius was in danger. While I stood looking at it the water rose from a small spring stream to a torrent, bearing rails, brush, and all movable stuff before it; the culvert became partially choked, and I saw that, unless speedily relieved, the bank would be washed away by that torrent. I rallied a number of men, and, with poles, and rails we jammed the brush and other obstructions through, and kept the culvert open until the rush was over, and the stream returned to its normal condition of a quiet brook. A dam breaking above had caused the rush of waters, and if we had not relieved the throat of the culvert, and the embankment had been washed out, the army would of necessity have fallen back, for it would have been impossible to have supplied it from Dispatch Station by teams, with the Virginia soil in its then soaked condition.

I quote from my diary: "Friday, June 6th. The transportation of the corps being ordered to the front, several wagons were lost in crossing the swamp, but none of mine. The roads are execrable, and even on the high ground and knolls, the wheels cut through frequently to the axles. Bad, almost impassable as the traveled track is, it is better than the apparently firm looking ground outside. Our march of seven miles occupied all day, and into the night — leaving some wagons fast in the mud within half a mile of camp. The newspaper generals in the great cities, with their granite pavements, are shouting themselves hoarse with the cry: 'On to Richmond!'

"Saturday, June 7th. I had a new road cut out through the woods by the Courtney house, and brought up everything left behind yesterday — a full day's work for all my men and teams.

"Sunday, the 8th. Our headquarters' tents are in a line parallel with and about ten feet from the ditch in which are buried the rebel dead. The rebels were advancing in force after driving Casey from his position, and were trying to get on his flank, when Dana's brigade, the advance of Sumner's corps, wheeled into line with

Kirby's battery, which had an oblique fire on the lane for a quarter of a mile. The lane, or road, was enclosed by a strong rail fence on either side, behind which the rebels were firing musketry. They had no artillery, or, if they had, did not bring it into action. When Kirby opened with spherical case and canister, rails and rebels were torn to pieces, and piled in a windrow. Dana then charged them in the woods, and Richardson, coming up on the right, drove them back to their line of defense and Fair Oaks was won. A ditch was dug parallel to the line of fences, and the dead rebels were covered as rapidly as possible, but not so deep but that the wagons crossing the ditch would sometimes cut through and turn up some parts of the buried bodies. Such are the horrors of war.

"Tuesday, the tenth of June. An east wind and picket firing roused us up as usual two or three times during the night. The enemy has brought up some artillery, and throws shells into our camp and beyond; no casualties reported as yet in our brigades, although shells have fallen in front, and behind, and into our camp. The stench of the shallow-buried bodies of union and rebel soldiers, and the unburied horses, is becoming unendurable, and the water for washing and drinking purposes is obtained by digging in the water soaked soil, and is nothing but surface water, which, if allowed to stand half an hour, becomes putrid. Our men are getting sick, and the surgeons say better advance and take the chances of battle than wait here for a certainty of death by disease."

Such scenes and memories of war are sufficient for the purposes of these recollections, and the recital of them will be avoided hereafter. On Wednesday we moved our camp back from this field of death.

XI

The Life of a Quartermaster

General Dana's camp was in a clump of trees near the railroad, back of the line of battle a short distance, and there I had a tent pitched. I was invited to join Dana's mess, in which was his adjutant Leach, a lawyer from my own town, and three aides whose names I do not now recall. The first time I met them at the table I do recall very distinctly. The table was the door of a stable or cowshed — or, as Dana said, of a hog pen — which the cook had wrenched from its place, made of rough boards, placed upon four stakes driven into the ground. The plates were of tin, badly marked by knives, and blackened by use; the coffee cups were common tin cups; the spoons were tin, the knives were poor iron, the forks were cast iron, and with many tines broken. The breakfast, or whatever meal it was I was invited to join them at, consisted of fried pork or bacon, swimming in grease. The coffee was black and muddy, the bread was hard tack. I looked at the layout with astonishment and disgust, but tried to eat something because I saw General Dana and Adjutant Leach do so as if they liked it. They broke into a laugh at my look of dismay, and shouted: "This is good enough food for soldiers, and it is all you will get! You may as well take kindly to it, and if you can't like it, run the mess yourself."

"Like it", I said, "like it, no; and what's more, I won't endure it. Surely it is not necessary, and it is not decent." I did run the mess. I sent to Washington, and had a camp table or two made with legs that folded. I ordered some white oil-cloth table covers, plated knives and forks, and a small table service of strong delft ware, and a supply of canned goods, dried fruit, and several cases of sardines in oil, twelve dozen in a case. These things, with some rough towels for the cook, and decent coffee pots and kettles, and the outfit was more satisfactory.

I heard of a farmer living in the woods about three miles on the north side of the Chickahominy who had sweet potatoes. I took a team and driver and started for the potatoes, crossing the river at the upper bridge. There I told an engineer officer of my purpose, and he went with me. We found the log house much farther away than I had supposed, and outside our lines. The farmer had the potatoes under the cabin floor, and charged three dollars a bushel for them, in gold. I took all he had to spare, and noticing that my friend, the engineer, was getting very uneasy, I started the teamster to go back the way we had come.

The engineer said: "I don't like the look of things here. I have been watching that woman, and I believe she has sent off to inform the rebels, and get them to capture us and the wagon. We are outside the lines, and they can take us if they try. If I were captured outside the lines it would ruin me. I am a regular, and supposed to know better; you are a volunteer, and not expected to know."

"Well, that's easy," I said. "We won't go with the wagon. We'll cut through the woods, and save half the distance."

"Won't we lose ourselves in this forest?"

"Lose nothing—" I answered; "I was brought up on the frontier, and can take you through the forest in a straight line, to your bridge."

We went at as rapid a gait as the horses could travel through the woods, brush, and down timber, and came out a few rods below his bridge, to his relief. The wagon with the potatoes came safely through, but much later. I had sweet potatoes in plenty— some for my friends.

I quote again from my diary:

"Tuesday, June tenth. Orders from General Sumner to keep a lookout for surprises; the enemy fired into and over our camp— as yet with no casualties. The stench from the dead again compels us to move camp. Around this camp are stacked many thousand boxes of ammunition, five feet high, covering an acre or two of ground. Should one of the shells the rebs are so frequently sending over here explode this mass, it would wipe our camp and all else off the face of the earth. The 19*th* and 20*th* Massachusetts are camped alongside.

"June 14*th*. I went to Whitehouse for supplies. The officer in charge was excited over the raid of Fitz Hugh Lee yesterday. He fired on a railroad train at Tunstall's station, killed some people, and wounded others on the train. Met my friend Senator Rice, of Minnesota, and Senator Harris, and Roscoe Conklin of New York. They had come down on a little steamer. After dinner with them on the boat, I took them to the White House (where Washington courted the widow Custis), and from there to the hospital. Senator Harris has a son, Lieutenant Harris, near here. These congressmen are here to call on General McClellan, and inform themselves personally of the condition of things at the front. 'I fear McClellan will be censured' one of them said, 'for putting a guard over the house, and for not putting the hospital in the yard of the place, — although it is better where it is.' And McClellan probably knew nothing of the guard, or of the location of the hospital, which is the Surgeon's business.

"June 21*st*. I took a detachment to the White House for stores, especially Johnson and Dow's patent cartridges. The Seventh Michigan used them in the battle of Fair Oaks, and the rebels thought they had repeating rifles."

On the twenty-fifth of June, General Hooker advanced his division, supported by Kearney on his left, pushed the enemy on the Williamsburg road, and Colonel Hinks, with the 19*th* Massachusetts, advanced through the woods and over the field beyond, until ordered back by Hooker. He came back with tears in his eyes, and said he could have run the enemy into Richmond.

The firing being very lively in front, I thought it would be becoming in me to join in the fight with General Dana, so I mounted and rode to where I had heard and supposed he was. I found him, and Adjutant Leach, and the aids, on foot in a clump of trees. As I rode up to them they did not seem at all pleased, and wanted to know what the devil I was there for, on horseback, so that the enemy would take me to be some major general, and concentrate a fire in that direction which would not be pleasant; my place, I was told, was to be with the transportation, where I would be ready to move as directed. As my company did not seem to be acceptable, I turned to go back by the same way I had come. Leach advised that I go by Hooker's camp, and not cross the rebels' line of fire, but I felt offended at being sent back, and rode back by the same way I had come and came very near being punished for my folly, for a shell from a large gun the rebs had mounted on a railway car came near taking my head with it as it plunged into the earth near by. Soon after the gun that threw that shell was dismounted by a shot from Pettit's battery and I was relieved from the apprehension of being blown up with our pile of ammunition.

The rebels had gathered troops from all quarters of the Confederacy for the defense of their capitol, and now, under the command of General Lee, they massed on our right to crush Porter's command, which was on the north side of the Chickahominy. Having learned, by Fitz Hugh Lee's cavalry raid, the position and condition of our base of supplies, they hoped to overwhelm Porter, and capture or destroy the supplies at White House. To meet this move McClellan had ordered the advance by Hooker which, if it had been pushed strongly, would have checked Lee's movement. But Hooker's attack on the defences of Richmond being withdrawn, Porter was driven across the Chickahominy, and McClellan obliged to change his base to the James River, and orders were given to load everything at White House, on vessels, and go to the James as rapidly as possible.

I was sent for to come to General Sumner's headquarters, to assume the duties of chief quartermaster, in place of Captain Putnam. When I reported to the General, he said: "Captain, we are getting ready to retreat, or to seek a new base, on the James River, and I want you to take charge of my transportation, and of the heavy artillery, and push them out of the way; it may be very important for me not to be delayed by the transportation."

"Certainly, General Sumner, I'll do the best I can, but I don't know as much about the business as Captain Bachelder, who has been here a long time. Would he not do the work better?"

The old gray haired General, with austere dignity, replied: "When I find it necessary to consult my inferior officers as to appointments, I will call on you, sir!"

I felt that somehow I had blundered, but did not then realize the honor done me in being selected for such important duty. I said: "Well, General, I am only a green volunteer, but please tell me where I am to take the transportation, and when I am to start."

"You will ride to General McClellan's headquarters, and ask these questions, and report to me as soon as possible."

To army headquarters I went, and saw Adjutant General Seth Williams. "I am sent by General Sumner," I told him, "to ask where I may take the transportation of the second corps, and when I may start."

"Our destination is the James River — by what roads I know not," he answered. "Better you see the chief quartermaster, General Van Vliet."

To him I went, and he knew nothing of the roads, and directed me to see the chief engineer, and he told me he had no map of the country, and knew nothing of the roads.

I reported to General Sumner, and said: "I will have to find a road, or make a road. The transportation is all ready. Shall I start them?"

"Not by my order. Get that from the Adjutant General, Seth Williams."

To him again I went, and by this time the engineer had heard of a narrow road through the woods leading south across White Oak Swamp, and advised that I take that road, on which teams were already moving. This road led by Savage Station, where immense piles of army supplies were stacked up to be fired, to prevent their falling into the hands of the enemy. I ordered my men to take on all they could carry of boxes of hard bread, and other supplies, and, finding the road leading south, pushed everything forward, and, before sundown, was well into this thicket of woods and brush.

The transportation of some of the troops that had been fighting on the north side of the Chickahominy was ahead of me, and made the delay that gave the opportunity to load some of my teams with supplies that were not receipted. The halting of a single wagon for any purpose checked the entire movement. There was no such thing as passing unless a new road was cut around the obstruction. The weather was damp. Soon a drizzle commenced which emphasized the darkness. After a halt longer than usual, I became impatient, and pushed my horse through the brush. Reaching the head of the train, I found a team halted, and the driver on the wagon asleep. I had to shake him violently to wake him, and he said he had run into something, and having been up and without sleep for two nights, he could not keep awake to find out what was the trouble.

I shaved some light bark from a tree, and, with some other light stuff made a fire on the ground, near the wagon that was fast. . . .

The light of my fire disclosed the difficulty and enabled the driver of the artillery wagon to back off, and resume the road. The trains being again in motion, I went forward until the swamp was reached just at break of day. I saw an artillery caisson to which four horses were attached, and the driver could get the discouraged team to move only a few yards at a time through mud which was up to the axle. I saw it would be impossible to get my train through that swamp, and ordered the wagon masters to park their wagons in an open field, which inclined toward the swamp, as fast as they came up, and to feed the animals. Then I rode back to a camp of engineers we had passed, and had the sentry wake the officer in command, and of him I asked questions about the swamp.

He had been sent, he told me, to build a bridge over the stream, so that the artillery could cross safely. His wagon of tools was down by the stream, and in it were axes to the use of which I could help myself. He said his men had been up so much of nights, and so pushed, that he must let them have some sleep and breakfast; after which he would bring them down to work; that a general in command of troops was camped on the other side of the creek, and that a good stone road was covered by trees that had been felled to obstruct it.

I rode back, struggled through the swamp, crossed the stream, and found the camp of the general (General Morrell, I think), who was wakened with difficulty to listen to my request for a detail of five hundred men, and my explanation of the necessity for the detail. He ordered it, and it was made immediately. We made short work of that quarter of a mile of big timber, and I soon had the transportation moving at as fast a gait as possible. The sticky places were the bridge, and the *débouché* on the south side, where the holes cut in the soft ground soon caused a stoppage. But I would not allow any halt to the movement across the bridge, and found it necessary sometimes to break the trains, greatly to the discontent of the officer in charge. A finely equipped train passing over was stopped by a leading team sticking in a mud hole. I ordered the teamster to pull to one side, and clear the bridge. A lieutenant on the other side hallooed to the driver to keep his place, not to break the train. I pricked up the mules with my sword, and compelled obedience to my order. When the lieutenant got across he was noisy with anger, and said: "This is General

McClellan's headquarters train, and I am a provost marshall, and I arrest you."

I said: "I care nothing for a headquarters train, or any other train. I know nothing of your power to arrest, but I know that this bridge has to be kept clear to save the lives of soldiers of the second corps, who are bringing up the rear. If you have any right to arrest me, you can't do it, but I will promise to report in arrest to the Commander-in-chief within twenty-four hours, and I promise further to give you a good, old fashioned, country licking the first time I meet you after I get clear of this more important duty. Now you get out of the way, and get out quick!" And he went.

I heard vociferous laughter, and looking round saw, seated on the grass a little way off, my engineer friend, (Alexander, I think his name was,) who had ridden with me after sweet potatoes, sitting near his grazing horse, laughing immoderately. I rode up to him, and said: "Something seems to have touched your funny bone — what is it?"

"Why," he replied, "I was sent here to keep this bridge clear, and to see you doing my duty so well tickles me."

"Well, you are here now," I said, "and you want to keep that bridge clear until the artillery is all over, and some of it in position on that rise just back of you, to protect this crossing. I'll leave you to enjoy your "tickle," while I go and find my own train that passed over some time back, and get something to eat and drink, as I have had nothing since yesterday morning."

The artillery did all get safely over, and none too soon. Tompkins' battery was placed on the ridge back of where I had left the engineer, and, after firing a few rounds, was ordered elsewhere, and another battery took its place, the commander of which was killed by a shot from Jackson's guns a short time after Tompkins left. So I was informed by Tompkins in A.D. 1894 or 95.

After leaving the engineer I remember nothing more until, before daybreak the following morning, I was wakened by Bachelder, who proposed we should ride out and explore a road. We soon mounted, and rode rapidly to the southwest. Seeing a farm house a little distant from the road, with two or three men on a porch, we rode up and made inquiry about roads, but meeting with unfriendly replies we turned and pursued our way to the forks of the road, where we met a Negro who gave us information readily. The Turkey Bend road directly south was the short way to the James River at Haxall's Landing; the road east was the Williamsburg Road; and that to the southeast the Charles City road. We cantered a short distance down the Turkey Bend road, and seeing two or three dead cavalry men by the roadside, turned and rode back toward our camp.

Passing some tents we saw General Marcy, chief of staff, whom I knew. Saluting, we asked for orders — where to take our transportation. General Marcy said: "We are going to the James River, but have no maps, no knowledge of the country or it's roads."

I dismounted and traced the roads we had seen in the dirt. While I was doing this General McClellan came and looked over the dirt map, and asked questions. Finally he said to march: "Pleasonton's cavalry must have gone down the road where they saw the dead cavalry men. I think it will be safe to let the trains go down the Turkey Bend road."

Then I said: "May we move at once? We are all hitched up, ready."

"I would like to have you ride with me, Captain," he said, "and show me where the roads meet."

"Very well, sir," I answered, "Captain Batchelder can start the trains — but I have had no breakfast."

"There is opportunity here for breakfast," he said. "I have just left the table, and some of my staff are yet there. Take your breakfast while my horse is being saddled." This being done we mounted and cantered off, accompanied by his orderly, who was a long way in the rear when we arrived at the cross roads. Here I pointed out the different roads, as explained by the negro, and he directed the movement of the transportation to be made down the road to Haxall's Landing. I remembered my controversy with the lieutenant in charge of his headquarters train, and my promise to report under arrest, and told the General I knew nothing about provost marshalls, or their authority, but did know that the bridge must be kept in use, or the Second Corps would suffer, and I did keep it clear, in spite of the complaints of officers in charge of trains.

"You were right, Captain," he said, "you are discharged from arrest, and I thank you for the valuable service you have rendered the army by clearing a passage across White Oak Swamp, and getting the transportation over."

"I did not stay to get it all over," I told him. "There was an engineer officer who came to my relief, and had charge when I left, but I would like to know the name of that lieutenant, for I promised him a good country thrashing, and I like to keep my promises."

"Let it pass, Captain, let it pass," he said. "Things are altogether too serious now to indulge in personal animosities."

XII

Retreat with the Army of the Potomac

I was looking at General McClellan as he spoke, and saw that he was much worried, and that this movement was a retreat to the James River, and not a flank movement to take Richmond, as I and others hoped and expected. Bachelder had started the trains, and brought them to the Turkey Bend Road down which we were moving, when I discovered men in line of battle, parallel with the road, and seeing General Dana, and Leach and others, I rode over to them, and learned that they were awaiting an attack from the enemy who were advancing, and that the trains were between the two lines of battle. The soldiers commenced calling and jeering "Get out of here — *git* — double quick!"

As the road was on a dry ridge, and was down hill, the drivers put whip to their teams, and raced down to the broad clover field on Malvern Hill, escaping with the loss of but one wagon of ammunition, hit by a shell. The hungry mules had only time for a few bites of clover when down came battery after battery of artillery, on the gallop, shouting: "Get out of here — we go into battery action here — get out — quick!"

They took the place, cutting me off from the road that led down and around the hill. To regain the Haxall road was the problem. It ran around the hill, and was plainly seen at the bottom of a very steep slope of a hundred and fifty or two hundred feet. There seemed to be no other way out of the difficulty and I dropped the entire train down the steep slope by locking both hind-wheels, and attaching a long picket rope to the axles of the foremost wagons, snubbed them down until a deep rut had been cut in the soft soil, then the rope was dispensed with. Some young trees on the brow of the hill afforded good snubbing posts, and the entire train went safely down with the upsetting of only two wagons. The drivers escaped serious injury. We made Haxall's before night of the 31st of June, the battle of Glendale or Nelson's Farm having been fought, and the enemy repulsed.

At Haxall's, while I was arranging my camp for the night, and getting something to eat, a newspaper correspondent made his appearance; "Gath," or George Alfred Townsend, riding bareback, on an abandoned rack of bones, a condemned army horse, wearing a bridle made of strings for a headstall, and reins, and a bit made from telegraph wire. He was made welcome, and in the morning departed on his Rosinante in search of material for his newspapers.

Late in the evening of the 31st the army headquarters tents were set up at the landing, and soon after General McClellan came, and went on board the vessel of Captain Rogers to consult with him (as was understood) as to the best place on the river for our supply station, and to direct him as to the position of our troops and the forces of the enemy, so that his fire from the gun boat should be effective in the coming battle. The immense one hundred pound shells made a fearful noise as they crashed through the tree tops, and the explosion was frightful. One among the first fired exploded at the front of a column of rebel troops that were forming to make a charge on our position, and did much to discourage the rebel soldiers. In the morning of July 1st, I collected my trains and started south. At about eleven o'clock I was ordered to march to Harrison's Landing, seven miles distant. Here camp was made, and tents pitched on the bank of the river, and when General Sumner arrived utterly exhausted, he lay down in my tent to rest, and fell asleep.

The Harrison and Westover plantations joined, and occupied some miles of the rich bottom lands that bordered the river, hundreds of acres of which were in wheat, ripe for the harvest, and the cutting of which had begun, much to the comfort of such soldiers as could secure bundles for their bedding. The uncut grain was used for the same purpose as far as possible. The rain had made the ground very soft, and it was not long before the fields were continuous areas of mud, made so by the tramping of the animals, vehicles, and men.

The enemy had followed us with a small detachment of troops, and a small battery, but were soon driven back to find safety in their own army, which was engaged in burying the dead at Malvern Hill. The repulse of the rebels there was so disastrous to them that the ablest officers of our army were opposed to any further retreat, but wanted to turn upon them, and drive them into Richmond. After the battle, Generals Sumner, Hooker, Kearney and others, were together on the porch of the Malvern House when the order to retreat to Harrison's Landing was received. Sumner said: "We have gained a great victory — I will not retreat farther."

Kearney was violent in denunciation, and exclaimed: "I tell you, gentlemen, this is either treason or cowardice!"

Hooker said: "Oh, no, Kearney — we will obey the orders of the commander-in-chief, whatever we may think."

The French soldier, the Duc d'Aumale, said to one of McClellan's staff: "Congratulate the General for me, and say that the time to move on Richmond is now."

The advice of Captain Rogers who thought the best place for the base of supplies was where the river was wider, seven miles below, governed. I have no doubt that he regretted afterward making the move *when* he did, for the position at Malvern was impregnable against any attack the rebels could have made at that time. After they had buried their dead, they retired to Richmond to reorganize, leaving a small body of troops at Malvern which General Hooker was ordered to drive away. This he did with little trouble, and held possession of the place for a few days, and returned to his camp near Harrison's.

I was ordered to take him some supplies while at Malvern, and it was one of the hottest days I ever experienced. I lost one teamster, and was prostrated myself by the heat. Fortunately it was near the house of Hill Carter, on whose porch I was laid, and was administered to by Mrs. Carter, with some restorative, and after a few hours was able to go on again, and report to General Hooker, who, in his shirt sleeves, was on the porch of the Malvern house, trying to keep cool. Here I commenced an acquaintance and friendship with General Hooker — one of the ablest soldiers and most lovable men it has been my good fortune to know — which continued through life.

When the army reached Harrison's, our surgeon, Doughty, took possession of the Harrison house for hospital purposes. This famous old colonial mansion was the birth place of President William Henry Harrison. When Doughty took possession of the house, he found that others had been there before him, and had carried off old and valuable letters and papers. He peremptorily stopped looting, and made the thieves he could hear of return what they had, and while we were there everything was scrupulously preserved and left in place. The house may have been left in the care of servants. Had the family remained at home a guard would have been put on the house, and nothing lost.

I had been changed from Dana's staff to Sumner's, and was ordered by him to seize all the corn and hay, or other supplies needed for army use, and give receipts to owners that might entitle them to a settlement in the future. Two brothers named Rowland had emigrated from New Jersey, and built a small mill, with modern machinery for making flour or meal. This mill was situated on a small creek which had given us much trouble in our crossing, in our march from Haxall's.

I quote from my diary of July second, 1862:

"Rain, and the passage of hundreds of wagons has worked the six inches of dust into mud, and, in places, in the brick-clay soil, there are two feet of adhesive mud. The condition of the soldiers marching through this in the rain was pitiable. The transportation was crowded on the farm of William Harrison, the wagons struggling for precedence over the narrow bridge that spanned Rowland's Creek, which was almost afloat. The engineers were busy with the pontoons building another to take the place of Rowland's Bridge, when that should become useless. The tangle and confusion were indescribable, and there was almost a panic among the drivers. I had the transportation of one brigade behind, in the rear of the entire line of transportation, and with others, it must take hours before it could get to the bridge — but it did not come. I rode back to find the cause of the delay, and found the movement obstructed by an overloaded one-horse ambulance driven by a boy; both horse and boy were exhausted. The road, on each side, was occupied by lines of wet, bedraggled soldiers, marching doggedly through the mud. I appealed to them to give a helping hand to the boy to unload the ambulance and get it out of the way of the trains, but they were wet, muddy, and miserable, and would not stop. I had to unload the ambulance myself, and I pitched the stuff out in the mud." . . .

When I returned to camp that night I found General Sumner and his adjutant and one aid, no others of his staff having come up, — the General utterly exhausted. He asked me if I could ride out and find Sedgewick and Richardson, and tell them where to find him. This I did, having gotten a fresh horse, and riding back and forth across the fields of Berkley and Shirley, I found Sedgewick, and from him learned the position of Richardson, and told them where General Sumner was. Dana I found sitting on a sheaf of wheat, and sick. I gave him my canteen, which had some commissary whiskey in it, and he took a good long pull, and repeated as did also his staff officers before I left. The rain never ceased; the wheatfield in which the troops were, was tramped into a field of mortar. I went back to my camp too tired to eat, and turned in for a night's sleep. I quote again from my diary:

"Thursday, the 3rd of July. Busy getting my trains together. The enemy shelled us from the hills, but General Kimball drove them off, and, it was reported, captured their guns.

"July 4th. I moved out to Rowland's Mills, and under orders of General Sumner, took possession of it, and finding two millers in the ranks, I set them to grinding the grain, and issued it only on the surgeon's order for the hospital. The army celebrated the fourth of July, mildly, by firing a national salute.

"Sunday, July 6th. Sent my clerk, C. A. Bronson, to Baltimore, with dispatches. General Dana is quite ill, with Chicahominy fever, he thinks. He seems beyond recovery, and is occasionally wandering in his mind. We put him aboard a steamer, and sent him to Philadelphia, in charge of his adjutant, Leach. President Lincoln arrived, and visited the camps.

"July 15th 1862. Visited the famous colonial mansion, Westover, the property and residence of John Seldon, to inquire into the amount of forage obtainable. . . .

"I found that some disorderly soldiers had made free with the corn and fodder of Mr. Seldon's, and had killed some of the fowls, hogs, and cattle, and Mrs. Seldon had put the remaining chickens in the basement of the mansion, and had the bacon left in her smoke house carried to the attic. Two cows were pastured in the front yard. I was pleased to inform her that my duty did not require that I should take, for army use, anything that was hers; that she had not enough left to supply her household and servants for the ninety days allowance I was permitted to leave. As I was about to take my departure, a woman sevant announced dinner, and Mrs. Seldon invited me to dine with them — an invitation I accepted with pleasure.

"A long table was set in a large dining room on the east side of the house, and the dinner consisted of a corn pone at one end of the table, and a dish of bacon and spinach at the other. We had, I think, a pudding. There was evidently a paucity of food, but no remark was made — no excuse for anything — we ate the dinner and were thankful. I enjoyed it, and shortly after took my leave." . . .

I copy from my memorandum book of date August, 14*th*, 1862.

"Have been quite unwell since Malvern Hill 2, scarcely able to be about the camp. Buried Chris Brubaker, one of my best teamsters. There being no chaplain in camp, I read the funeral service myself, and saw him decently buried in a grave. We are under marching orders, and have been for a week. It is now understood that we go to Fortress Monroe —

"Friday, August 15*th*, 1862. General Sumner this morning ordered me to take charge of the trains, and push them through, intimating very clearly that he had no confidence in P——. The route, after passing Charles City, is to the right, and across the Chickahominy toward the mouth, then by way of Williamsburg and Yorktown to Fortress Monroe." . . .

We crossed the Chickahominy on a pontoon bridge near its entrance to the James, and encamped on the east side on Sunday, and I held the train subject to the orders of General Sumner. General Burnside, coming up the river on a tug, landed and enquired why we delayed, as we were all hitched up ready to move. I told him that I was waiting orders from General Sumner. He advised that we push on, as undoubtedly the troops would find us in their way if we delayed longer. An aid from General McClellan then came, and ordered all trains to push forward to Fortress Monroe as soon as possible. This we did, camping that night four miles from Williamsburg, in which famous old town Captain Bachelder and I hired a Negro cook to prepare for us a good dinner. We were anxious lest the troops would want rations, and we left wagons with two days rations, and pushed on with the remaining transportation. We left Yorktown to the left, and halted nineteen miles from the Fortress to feed; left again at seven in the evening, and at two A.M. encamped near the Seminary Hospital with the greater part of the train.

On the 23rd General Sumner took me to task for marching the train so rapidly, and wanted to know by whose orders I had presumed to push so far in advance of the troops. I replied "First by your own orders, then by direction of General Burnside, and then by order of General McClellan." Whereupon he said, "You were right, but if it had not been for a special dispensation of divine Providence, in the shape of a herd of cattle, my men would have starved."

For some days I was sick with a fever, and in the care of Surgeon Hand, but I would not go to the hospital. When the troops were shipped on vessels, and ready to depart, General Sumner sent for me, and said he wished me to remain and forward the transportation to Aquia Creek Landing, or wherever he might be found. I said I was on the sick list, but would do the best I could, and if he would leave me some men for extra duty it would help. He said he would leave me five hundred, but when they reported there were only fifty. Part of the time I had my bed carried out on the dock, and gave orders from there. On the 27th a drunken wagon master took one of my mules. I ordered it taken away from him, and he was so fool-drunk that he drew a pistol to shoot me, as I lay on my bed. Lieutenant Gleason, A.A.Q.M., happened to be near him, and choked him, and pinned him to the earth, until the guard gathered him in, and took him to the guard house.

XIII

With the Eleventh Corps

There was inexcusable mismanagement in transferring the Army of the Potomac from the James River to the vicinity of Washington. With all the resources of the government placed in the hands of the officers it should have been transferred from Newport News to Alexandria or Washington, and landed in as good order as that in which it embarked, each corps by itself, with its own transportation accompanying it, and within two weeks. Instead of that a period of six weeks was occupied, and everything was scattered, and had to be collected again for each corps. Vessels and barges were employed, the demurrage on which was more than the value of the vessels and barges. My plan was, the vessel being ready, to drive down team number one — a man on each side, with a paint pot and marking brush; unhitch the team, and take them out of the way — i.e. ship them, with driver to care for them, on the proper vessel; mark the wagon tongue number one, also each wheel and axle, on each side, the right side red, the left blue, and the wagon body the same — each as fast as marked to be carried on board ship, and, when unloaded, the action reversed, and the same team hitched onto their old wagon.

It was the tenth of September when I commenced to unload the transportation of the second corps at Alexandria and Georgetown, and at the ordnance wharf in Washington. Assembling the trains, and loading with supplies, I hastened them forward through Poolsville, Frederick, Boonsboro, to near Keedysville, and rode forward to witness the great battle of Antietam. I saw Generals McClellan and Porter talking together, and approached to await

94

an opportunity to ask where I would find General Sumner. Porter was receiving directions to support Burnside's attack on the enemy's flank at the bridge, and the tardiness with which he moved was very noticeable. I wondered that McClellan did not say something that would have quickened his motions. In reply to my inquiry he said General Sumner would be found on the right, and was then engaged in battle. To the right I went, behind the lines of battle, and when I found the old warrior the firing had ceased, and the enemy were defeated, with great loss on both sides. I reported the arrival of the train with supplies and amunition, and some one of the staff having said "Your friend Dana is wounded" I asked where I might find him. General Sumner said "The surgeons will look after your friend, — your place is with your command; and be ready to move forward or to the rear, as ordered." Of course I went, and without delay, but when the evening shades were falling and it was apparent that the fighting was over for the day, and the ambulances were bringing in the wounded to the temporary hospitals at Keedysville, I looked around for any wounded friends. Sedgewick, Dana, Audenried, and Devereaux I found in one house; I took messages from all who wished me to and went to the telegraph office for my turn at the wire. General Sedgewick, who's wound was in the forearm and wrist and very painful, said: "No, I have no message to send. I have no wife nor child, nor will I annoy any friends. Here I remain until this is fought out." He thought there would be a continuation of the battle next day, but the rebels had had enough and were retreating across the Potomac.

The battle field was an awful spectacle to show in the light of that quiet morning sun next day, forty-six years ago. The memory of it is painful. Let it be buried with the other tragedies of that fratricidal contest as something too horrible to think about. When the dead were buried out of sight we followed the rebels across the Potomac, and the second corps was encamped at and near Harper's Ferry to refit. General McClellan was censured much for neglecting to pursue the rebels vigorously, and the dissatisfaction felt and manifested in the country and in congress led to his removal and the appointment of General Burnside to the chief command of the army of the Potomac; and this against his protest that he was not capable of commanding so large an army. This was soon manifest in the disastrous Fredericksburg campaign which destroyed all confidence of the soldiers in their commanders, and weakened their faith in the government.

During our encampment on Bolivar Heights * when the second corps was refitting and receiving some reinforcements, a newly enlisted regiment camped near my tents, and their cook, in making a fireplace for his camp kettle, picked up some stones, and, among other things, a round cast-iron ball, which he used with the stones to place his kettles and coffee pots on. His fire was scarcely hot when this shell exploded; fortunately it did not kill the man, but it taught him to avoid shells when possible thereafter.

General McClellan's headquarters were across the river a few miles from Harper's Ferry, and hearing that Bishop McIlvaine was to preach there one Sunday, I rode over to pay my respects to my venerable friend of college days. While there I met Colonel Colby, of McClellan's staff, and in conversation with him about our experience on the Peninsula, he said the General had often inquired if any one could tell him the name of the officer who had planked the railroad bridge over the Chickahominy, and who had cleared out the White Oak Swamp road. He advised me to send a statement to Headquarters. This I did, claiming to have saved twelve or eighteen hours at White Oak Swamp, thereby saving a position at Malvern Hill, and the heavy artillery, &c. Shortly after I had a note from General Ingalls informing me that I would be promoted to the first vacancy. . . .

I soon received notice of my appointment as chief quartermaster of the eleventh corps, commanded by General Sigel, and I reported at his headquarters, at Gainsville, Virginia. I had received the appointment through General Ingalls, the chief quartermaster of the Army of the Potomac, who told me the affairs of the quartermaster of the corps were in bad shape, and so I found them. The former quartermaster had died, and the business had been entrusted to an aide-de-camp, who signed the necessary vouchers prepared by the clerk of the former quartermaster. This clerk appeared to be the tool of the chief of staff, Lieutenant Colonel A———, a smart, vulgar fellow, who had been a policeman, so he said. He entertained me on the first night of my introduction to the staff by telling me how he and others had blackmailed a respectable citizen, and got from him five hundred dollars; and this scoundrel was chief of staff! Of course there was trickery to be

* Near Harper's Ferry.

expected where he was. The Adjutant General was Lieutenant Colonel Mysenburg, a respectable young German from St. Louis, who attended to his duties faithfully. Another German on that staff was a Major ———, an engineer, who had detailed for his use wagons supposed to be loaded with army supplies, which, on the march, I found overloaded with personal supplies for the Major; barrels of apples, a barrel of whiskey, and all sorts of comforts and conveniences for himself. In a movement of troops, the overloaded wagon having stopped the trains, I had occasion to overhaul it, and set the barrels of apples on the roadside, turned over the whiskey to the hospital department, and notified him that his transportation must be limited to the regulation allowance. I informed General Sigel that the Major's ways of doing things were not useful ones; that he was in the way, and on the march wholly unnecessary; and he was sent with his compass and chain and his drawing boards elsewhere. I kept enlisted men detailed for his purposes, and made of them a pioneer company to clear out obstructions, and corduroy the roads when necessary. These men soon became expert road repairers, and corduroy builders, of great assistance in the winter in Virginia, where we had frequently to pass our trains over the country roads. This was the case when we moved to Stafford, and had to move supplies from a station which I established on the Potomac River, not far from Aquia Creek Landing. The road soon became impassable, and had to be corduroyed in all low wet places. I had to makes miles of corduroy — felling the pine and other trees, and laying parallel logs eight feet apart, putting on a cover of cross logs notched down to as near a level as was convenient, and shoveling in the dirt from each side, making a ditch to secure drainage.

To the Eleventh Corps was added the Twelfth, and this was called the Reserve Grand Division, and was under the command of General Franz Sigel. The camps were three and four miles from where I received supplies at the river station. The clerk at the river station sent me word one day that there was a boat load of oysters there, and asked if I would like to buy some. I sent him word to buy all the boatman had, and send them up to camp. I supposed a boat load of oysters was six or eight bushels — as many as would be carried in a little boat or skiff, and thought I would indulge myself. My surprise may be imagined when that afternoon two or three wagons drove up to my camp, with notice that other like loads were following. It appeared I had bought a schooner load (twenty tons) of the desirable bivalves, and what to do with them was a pressing question. I started the teams through the camps, selling the oysters at cost to officers and soldiers, who gave the quartermaster great credit for his thoughtfulness.

In February the Reserve Grand Division was dissolved, with General Sigel in command of the Eleventh Corps. This being unsatisfactory to him, he was relieved, and a West Point graduate, who, before the war, had abandoned the military profession, and was preparing himself for the Episcopal ministry, was appointed to the command of the corps. He brought with him his brother Charles, and a Major Whittlesey as aid, and a chaplain, Alvord, who kept the newspapers full of the glory of "the Havelock of America" O. O. Howard. The officers and soldiers of the Eleventh Corps who had been accustomed to the alert, soldier-like ways of General Sigel, did not approve of what seemed the attempt of General Howard to make a Sunday School class of a military organization, and his conduct at Chancellorsville and Wauhatchie satisfied them that he was not fitted to command even a regiment in active duty against an enemy. He was always ready to encounter personal danger when duty required, but appeared more concerned with saving the souls of his men and of the enemy, than with the care of their bodies, and was wanting in that first requisite of a general, an intuitive knowledge of men, and an appreciation of their abilities. He was ready to obey orders when under the direction of his superior, but lacked initiative in meeting emergencies. By officers and men he was regarded as a tin soldier; by the church people generally, because of Parson Alvord's newspaper articles, he was thought to be a great hero.

June the tenth, or thereabout, I suggested to General Hooker the use of fire engines in breaching the walls at Vicksburg, before which Grant had been pounding away, and had his parallels up so close that hand grenades were thrown over the walls. He said that it could undoubtedly be made successful, and that I might take a run up to Washington, and suggest it to Headquarters there. I went to Halleck's Headquarters, and there saw Colonel Kelton, who also approved. Then I went to Alexandria, and obtained the use of a little fire engine with which to experiment, on a bank of indurated clay in that city; the result was satisfactory, and I proposed to go out with engines obtained in Cincinnati

and St. Louis, and wash a breach in the walls; but before the arrangements were completed Pemberton was starved out, and the
place surrendered.

As we were marching through Maryland, and camped for a
day at Middletown, I was seized with an inflamation of the sino-
vial membrane in the left shoulder, which paralized the left arm,
and the surgeons sent me to the hospital at Washington for treatment. Here I was in the hands of Doctor Clymer and some others
who blistered my shoulder, and, when I was able to get about with
my arm in a sling, came word from the front of the meeting of the
enemy, and of Reynolds' death. I started on the next train for
Gettysburg, and got there on the day of the last repulse of the
rebels, and was ordered to put my trains in a defensive position,
awaiting an attack from the enemy's cavalry under Stuart, said
to be working round our rear to cut off transportation. I barri-
caded the approaches by the traveled roads, placed two pieces of
Diedrick's battery in commanding positions, and awaited the result. Fortunately no enemy appeared. He had learned of the
defeat of Lee's assault, and hastened back to the lines of the rebels.
He covered the rear of the rebel army that fled to the Potomac at
Williamsport. Meade let them march without annoyance, and
camp, and fortify a camp on the Potomac.

The battle field of Gettysburg I do not wish to remember. I
visited the hospital where were the Colonel and Lieutenant
Colonel of the First Minnesota, and found them so desperately
wounded that I never expected to see them again, but both lived
to engage in active business at home.

The Army of the Potomac followed up in a leisurely way, and
camped, and fortified their camp, waiting for Lee to escape across
the Potomac. The soldiers were anxious to go in and make an
end of the war, and go home. They could not understand such
generalship, and became very impatient. Heavy rains had washed
the Potomac to half flood tide, and the rebels could not cross until
they could make pontoons. Lee, as everyone knew, was short of
supplies of all kinds, food, forage, and ammunition. The soldiers
said: "If Hooker had been left in command we would end this
thing here and now; but Meade is an accidental victor, and is
afraid he will lose some reputation; he says he is waiting to 'get a
good ready'."

The authorities at Washington urged the attack, but Meade

seemed anxious to have Lee escape to the other side of the Potomac, on the way to Richmond. I proposed to Howard that he get permission from Meade to let me take a regiment of Minnesota or Wisconsin troops, and go around Lee's army, up the Potomac, and cut down trees, leaving the limbs on, so that, when tumbled into the rapid river, they would make it impossible to lay or keep a pontoon bridge. This until Meade had had time to "get his good ready". Howard went to Meade to get permission, and Meade told him it was a good military maxim to make a bridge for a flying enemy.

Lee tore down houses, and with such lumber as he could get made pontoons, and crossed his army over the river safely to meet his supplies and reinforcements coming rapidly from Richmond; having met which, he turned around and offered battle – an offer Meade dared not accept. Thus ended the battle inaugurated by the brilliant strategy of General Hooker, and his skillful handling of the Army of the Potomac until it was in position at Gettysburg, – where Hooker, with his finger on the map months before, when Lee started north, had said: "If Lee crosses the Potomac, as it seems he will be compelled to do, there, or in that neighborhood, will be fought, the great battle of the war." And there it was fought.

The Army of the Potomac, as a unit, under the orders of Hooker, met, in a favorable position, the Army of Virginia, under command of their most skillful leader, and won the victory before Meade had time to change the position of the different corps. He wished to retreat to what he thought a more favorable battle ground – called a council of war – had no confidence in himself or the army. He had not made it; Hooker had. The victory was to Meade's credit accidentally, as the soldiers said. They believed that, had Hooker been in command, Lee's army would never have recrossed the Potomac, except as prisoners. There are those who think the removal of Hooker at that time providential, because if Lee's army had been destroyed or captured then the rebels, not yet ready to give up, might have desolated the country for years with a guerrilla war. It required the work of Grant and Sherman to finally subdue them. . . .

On September 23rd, 1863, sudden and unexpected orders were received to march to Alexandria, and take rail transportation for some destination unknown; the transportation, the mules, to be turned in to the depot quartermaster at Alexandria. This order was a most unnecessary blunder. Who was responsible for it? I do not know whether it was General Meiggs or Ingalls; I protested against it in vain. Our disciplined, well broken mules were taken from us, and we were told to reorganize our transportation at Nashville. The corral there was supplied with broken down and young, unbroken mules — colts. These were issued to my teamsters to break in and use in crossing the mountains of Tennessee. Many of them died in the mountain roads. My good serviceable mules were finally shipped out to Nashville to supply the place of those issued to me, and were retained there to work in the city. The teams should have been shipped in care of their drivers.

The Eleventh and Twelfth Corps, commanded by General Hooker, were sent to Tennessee to help Rosecrans. The latter, having by brilliant strategy, and the desperate battle of Chicka-mauga, won the position at Chattanooga, was now in danger of losing it for want of supplies. The two army corps were distributed from Nashville to Bridgeport, with headquarters at Stevenson. I was stationed at Bridgeport, at which place I arrived October 3rd, at eight o'clock. Owing to the destruction of the railroad bridge across the Tennessee River at this place the trains could run no farther, and in fact the base of supplies was Stevenson, twelve miles west of Bridgeport. A supply train of seven hundred wagons had been employed to carry rations to Chattanooga by a long moun-tain road, but it was hardly possible to feed and supply the army in this way. Rosecrans had ordered three little flat-bottomed steam-boats to be built at Bridgeport, and had left a quartermaster, named Edwards, with instructions to push the work. Edwards had been the captain of a little steam vessel running from Sandusky to Detroit, and had brought a ship carpenter from some lake port to take charge of the building, whose name was Turner — a compe-tent mechanic.

Turner had the frame of a scow flat-boat on some oak blocks set on end by the river side; this he was planking and getting ready for the engine of a small stern-wheel craft, taken apart at Nashville, and to be shipped to Bridgeport. The Sunday after our arrival General Howard heard some hammering on the boat, and sent an order to stop all work on Sunday, to the astonishment of the workmen and all others who knew that men's lives depended on the speedy use of that boat. I took good care that no further interruption of work occurred — day or night or Sunday — by getting a positive order from higher authority.

I quote from letters to my wife, and from my diary. "It rained heavily, and the water rose eight feet. In the afternoon" (of the 15th or 16th) "feeling anxious about the hull of the boat, I went down to see the condition of things, and found the water rising rapidly, and Turner anxious and afraid the hull would be floated off the blocks; he was weighting it down with pig iron, a lot of which had been left by the rebels. 'That won't do, Turner,' I said, 'if it gets wet you can't caulk it until it gets dry. We must save the hull, or build a new one.' I asked where the Captain was, and was told he had gone to his tent, having given it up.

"I went to the Captain's tent, and found him lying in his bunk, overcome with work and worry and disappointment. He had been getting telegrams all day about the boat, and was utterly discouraged. He couldn't save the boat he told me. As I came out of his tent I saw several flat-boats that had been used in making a pontoon bridge. They were tied up to the bank. I started on a run for the boat-yard, and as I approached called to Turner to throw off the pig-iron, and get all the buckets in camp, and have some carpenters bore holes in the pontoon flats to let them fill with water as they were floated down to where they could be gotten under the boat, — when the holes could be plugged, and the water dipped out of them with buckets. There was at this time only eighteen inches below the hull, and the water was rising fast."

Turner was satisfied that this plan would do, and the pontoons were brought down. He called for a man to come into the water with him to knock out the blocks that were holding up the boat. One of them followed him in, and I started men to get the buckets ready to dip the water out of the pontoons when they had been pulled under the hull. We had some difficulty in getting the hull balanced properly on the pontoons, but it was done, — supported safely on four pontoons.

The work on the boat was pushed day and night until she was ready to launch, with the engine and machinery put in place. I had her run above the bridge before the smoke stack was put in place. Two of the pontoons were loaded with rations, and the little Chattanooga made her trial trip, towing them up the river to meet a division of troops that had left Chattanooga to forage on the country until they could reach supplies at Bridgeport. The soldiers were skirmishing through the fields after rabbits, birds, or anything for food, when they discovered the approaching steamboat, and coming to the river bank, raised a shout: "Hurrah for the bully little steamboat! Rations once more — hurrah!"

When the pontoons touched the shore they jumped aboard and commenced to throw off the boxes of hardtack, bacon, and the like, regardless of the commissary in charge, who shouted out: "Don't do that, boys — I have to account for all this stuff!"

"All right, Captain, our commissary can give you receipts to burn. Pull down that fence, and make a fire — here's coffee and sowbelly, and hardtack once more — hurrah for the bully little steamboat — rah, rah, rah!"

A pontoon being left with the rations the steamer returned from her first trip to load and carry supplies to General Hooker, at Kelly's Ferry, and for the troops at Chattanooga, then on their last few boxes of hardtack. Having loaded two pontoons — which were not the regular sized pontoons, but small barges or flats that had been used as pontoons, and were capable of carrying twenty-five to thirty thousand rations — and put a deck load on the Chattanooga, I started up the Tennessee River to land them at Kelly's Ferry, three miles from Hooker's camp, and twelve miles from Chattanooga. I had found among the troops but one man, Williams, who claimed to know how to manage a steamboat from the pilot house. He said he had run a steam ferry-boat between Cincinnatti and Covington, I had myself some little knowledge of steamboat bells, having been part owner and manager of a steam ferry-boat that plied between Hastings and Prescott, and I went myself with Williams into the pilot house, which was a temporary makeshift, put up on posts and braced from the deck, there being no upper works as yet. Williams knew the business very well. I had also a man who had been on the Arrow, on Lake Erie, with Captain Edwards, as mate. I put him on the bow, to watch for logs, or others drift, in this unknown, rising mountain river. There was but a light load on the deck of the hull, and, moving under a good head of steam against the current, there was too great vibration, and soon one of the hog-chains broke. These chains were of only three-quarter iron rods, the heaviest we could obtain. Having no anchor we drifted until it was fixed up with rope, and after losing an hour or more, we started up stream again, but with a less head of steam. After that we carried only enough steam to best the current, and crawl up this rapid river. We had another break, were again delayed, and again went on, but oh, how slowly! The night was dark, and the rain constant, and the mate on the bow was frightened out of his wits, and wanted to stop and tie up to shore, and when I refused and ordered him back to his place on the bow, he exclaimed: "If only I had my compass, so I could tell which way we are going!" This was greeted with a shout of derision, and: "Much good a compass would do you in this mountain stream you never saw before!"

Crawling along about midnight we came opposite to a campfire on the north bank, and a sentry on duty before the fire. I told Williams to keep over to the south shore as near as was prudent, as I didn't know of any of our troops on the north side, and these might be rebels. As we came opposite to the fire I shouted to the sentry: "What troops are those?" And the answer came back: "Ninth" (or some other) "Tennessee!" I said: "Crowd the south shore as near as you dare, Williams — I don't know of any such union troops." Then I shouted: "Who's your Colonel?" and he replied, reassuringly, that it was Stokes, and I knew there was a Tennessee Colonel Stokes on our side, and I shouted back to the sentry: "How far is Kelly's Ferry from here?" and he returned that it was up yonder where we saw the camp-fire.

We kept paddling along slowly, but safely, toward the fire on the south shore, and making a careful approach, tied up, and got out a plank, and I landed in the arms of my faithful assistant quartermaster, Joe Shoeninger, who hugged me, and hurried me through the rain to a sort of shelter, where he had a huge fire blazing, and where it was possible, by turning first one side and then the other, to get warm and partly dry, and then lie down on a plank to get some sleep; not, however, before I had had Shoeninger send a mounted man to tell General Hooker that the rations had arrived. As the messenger rode through the camps he told the sentries, and they woke up the sleepers, who hurrahed and shouted that the "Cracker line" was open. They made as much noise as if we had won a victory — as, indeed, we had. The next morning I rode over to camp and received the congratulations of Hooker, Howard, and the others. I supposed I would now be allowed to take my place as Quartermaster of the Eleventh Corps, and have an easier time.

XIV

At Bridgeport

Colonel James H. Wilson, of General Grant's staff, had been sent down to Bridgeport to inspect things at the rear, and went down the river with me in a pontoon boat, and, looking over affairs at Bridgeport, he saw what I had done, and I had orders from General Grant's headquarters to take charge at Bridgeport, and build up a depot of and for supplies. I was assigned to this duty by the following order: "Chattanooga, November 6th, 1863. Lieut. Col. Le Duc A. Q. M. 11th Corps, will proceed to Bridgeport and Stevenson, and superintend the erection of buildings at Bridgeport, and the removal of those at Stevenson. The work will be done as rapidly as possible without exposure of the stores at Stevenson, and material removed to Bridgeport as speedily as it can be done without interfering with the transportation of supplies. The site for the building will be selected today. The work on the ordnance building at Stevenson will be discontinued. By order of General Thomas.

"Wm. McMichael, A. A. Gen.
"To Lieut. Col. Le Duc, A. Q. M. through Lieut. Col. Wilson A. I. C."

Colonel Wilson and I went down together. Finding the Chattanooga had left Kelly's Ferry, we took a pontoon, and a detail of four soldiers, and rowed down as far as Shellmound, and there finding an old engine I had fixed for service, we took her, and finished our trip by rail, but with blistered hands from rowing. We looked the place all over, and decided on the location of side-track and buildings. Wilson returned to Chattanooga, but not before I told him he had done me a great disfavor. "Why, how is that?" he said. "This is the most important place just now, and there must be some one here who can and will do the work."

"Very true, but by taking me from the Corps you reduce my rank, and by reducing my rank you reduce my pay."

"No," he said, "that must not be; I will see to it that you do not lose by the change. General Grant can fix that."

"Well, he may, I hope," I answered, "but I doubt it."

I got as many men detailed for extra duty as possible each day, and, with such tools as were to be had, commenced the work. I sent to Minnesota, and brought down some good men that I knew: Byron and Felix Howes, for clerks, Cogshall, Stone, Truax, Sutliff Chiquet, and others I do not remember, who were first rate men as clerks, carpenters, mill men, or wherever employed. I seized and refitted some country sawmills I found, and brought in one or two portable mills, and had them all at work making oak lumber for my station buildings, and for the steamboats building, and for army use.

I will quote here some extracts from letters to my wife at about this time.

"Bridgeport, Nov. 8th, 1863. I came down here yesterday under orders to remain for the present, and to make this a large depot of supplies; to erect the necessary buildings, put in the railroad sidetrack, take command of the quartermaster's department, and 'put it through.'

"Nov. 10th. I am in my own tents again at Bridgeport, and expect to remain until a depot is built, and supplies gathered and forwarded to Chattanooga.

"Nov. 13th. Who do you suppose took supper with me this evening? Cump Sherman, and Audenried, whom I helped at Antietam, when he was wounded. Of course you know 'Cump' — alias General Sherman. He is looking rugged, and has, of course, grown older, but not any faster than myself. We were very glad to see each other, and had a pleasant time. He looked over my photographs — yours, and those of the children — and, as he remains here to collect his corps, I hope to see more of him, and to talk over old times, and school days. He is in command of the Army of Tennessee, and Frank Blair is in command of one corps. Audenried is asleep in my tent. He is a Philadelphia graduate of West Point, — a pleasant young fellow. They have put me in a very responsible place here, and expect very great exertions and very great results, they say. I hope not to disappoint them. My pay is reduced — which is wrong; it should be increased. I have cut loose from the Eleventh Corps. When you see the General's sister, Susan (my playmate in youthful days) tell her I think Cump one of the best generals in the world, and am proud of his name and fame. Hugh Ewing is his brother-in-law, you know. He is a lawyer in Kansas. Tom Ewing is a brigadier general, and passed over the river with his division yesterday. Charles is Lieutenant Colonel on Sherman's staff. Cump told me of the fate of some other Lancaster boys. John McCracken, son of the most wealthy man in Lancaster in my time, is a runner for a steamboat line. M—— H——, a fine classical scholar, and a good Presbyterian, is now a drunken beggar in Sonora — if alive. Bill —— died in Sonora, a deputy sheriff, a gambler, &c. Ed ——, (H——'s eldest son), is a border ruffian in California, and has been twice tried for his life. Once Sherman saved him from being hung by a mob. Almost everyone whose parents were wealthy has turned out badly, while those of poorer parents have made useful citizens.

"Nov. 20. My road to the river is nearly done. We will have the iron on it next week. The little stern-wheel boats (two of them) are doing good work, and supplying the army thus far tolerably well. We will have another soon — the Dunbar, which the rebels left at Chattanooga; a side-wheeler, with part of the machinery taken out, but we will have her running within five days. She is a swift and powerful boat.

"I am out soon after daylight, write up what letters and dispatches have come, get breakfast, mount a horse, and am not much in my tent until night. First I go to the steamboat landing to see if they are pushing forward the stores; next to the railroad station, to see what goods have arrived, and if the teams are loaded promptly, and sent to their proper destination. Next to the sawmills, to note the lumber on hand; next to the ship yard, to note progress on the steamboat, and hurry the work if possible; then to look after the coal-pit, and the new buildings; then, perhaps, to the other side of the river to look after a train of cars I have made up on that side. Having found an engine that had been in use in a coal mine, and had been run into the mouth of the mine, and had a part of the cylinder taken away, I sent to Nashville, had the missing part made and replaced, and so have an engine on the other side of the river usefully employed, and, when the bridge is finished, will bring it on this side, for a switch engine. Having gone through all this once or oftener, and having arranged the business of tomorrow, then I have supper, and reports — letters and such — until ten or eleven o'clock, or later, as the exigencies of the work may require. Then I snatch a few hours sleep, and begin it all over again in the morning."

I find a memorandum which I copy here, showing only one sample of the activities of the times:

"On the 8th I took Major McA———— and his regiment, and twenty-five cavalry of the Fifth Tennessee, and went after some forage down to the mouth of Island Creek. I posted the infantry around a field of corn, and sent the cavalry up the mountain as videttes and scouts. They brought in Major H. S. Williams, of the 9th Alabama Infantry, James H. Bill, and David Tams, also two pieces of rebel cloth (gray — army pattern), three shot guns, one rifle, one sabre, one Colt's revolver, one musket, and one pair of army boots. After loading the wagons with corn we returned safely to camp.

"The Chattanooga came down, and reported the swamping of a barge with the men and baggage of the 33rd Jersey, and some men drowned, and some baggage lost through the incompetence of Captain D————, who is wholly unfit for the command of any boat on the river. He had experience as mate on a little ferry boat on Lake Erie, but knows nothing of river navigation, and is incapable. Employed by Edwards, whose mate he had been."

Sometime in the latter part of November, or in December, in launching the Chicamauga, she stuck fast in the mud, and Turner, the ship carpenter, had the Dunbar hitch on a two inch new hawser to pull her off. The Dunbar broke up five feet of deck, broke the hawser, and the hull remained fast in the mud. As there were several squared oak timbers, twelve by twelve inches, and twenty to thirty feet long, I suggested to Turner to hollow the end of one, and round the end of another; place one end against the end bow of the hull, and the other end of a broken lever against a convenient stump; attach block and tackle to the joint, and two men and a boy would shove her off. The power of the broken lever, where there is opportunity to employ it, is irresistable. On another occasion I was sitting on the bench in Turner's drafting room while he was employed in drafting some lines for a speedy running

Toward eleven or twelve o'clock, as I was sitting with my hat drawn down to partly conceal my face, and with my common blue overcoat drawn around my shoulders, I noticed a man in a major's uniform, wearing glasses, and with an unmistakeably German face, who came to the desk and scanned closely the register of arrivals. (I had thought it better not to register.) He turned away smoking a cigar, and I thought I knew him for a man who had been a clerk of mine in St. Paul, in 1854. When he left the room, I took occasion to ask the proprietor, — whose name was Miller, I think — the name of the officer who had gone out.

"That is Major Helvita. He is from Lexington, in this state. He is an officer in a regiment of Kentucky cavalry, has seen some service, and been captured twice, and got away. He is on the court martial trying Generals Buell and Crittenden in this city."

"What did he do for a living before he entered the army?"

"He was a music teacher in Lexington, and here sometimes."

"Did you ever hear him play the piano? Does he play in this manner?" and I gave an illustration of his playing.

"Yes, yes, that's it. What do you know about him?"

I said I thought I had seen him somewhere, years ago, and changed the conversation. I wished to be thoroughly satisfied, and waited for him to come to his breakfast the next morning, when I followed him into the room, taking a seat where I could observe his actions, and I saw him sit down, giving two little hitches to his chair, and bend his head — for he was near sighted — over the bill of fare. I was careful to leave the table before he did, and take my seat guarding my money box, (relieving my orderly) and wait for the Major to come out and light a cigar, and take the two little puffs that accompanied that action. This he did, as I expected, and then I knew him to be the man who, by breach of trust when in St. Paul, had robbed a friend of ten thousand dollars deposited in a bank, had married a Miss D ———, and gone to Germany with his bride, and with the stolen money. The bride's father, a German official, had hurried his son-in-law out of reach of German authority (it appeared that he had done something in Germany that had made him liable to arrest if he returned there) into Italy, and from there he went to England, where his wife joined him. Then he had come back to America, and up the Lakes to Superior City, Wisconsin. In some way the banker had heard of him there, and sent the sheriff after him, but he disappeared as soon as the sheriff — who was well known to him — arrived in town. The sheriff brought the wife through to St. Paul, and the adventurer was lost until I found him, in the garb of Major Helvita on the court marshall in Louisville. I had learned that he had been a teacher of music in New York State; and also editor of a German paper in a political campaign. His wife obtained a divorce, in which I believe he was debarred from marrying again. Many years after the war I sat in a seat with a gentleman who said he lived in Lexington, Kentucky. I asked if he knew a Major Helvita. He said he had known him for years, and that he was a teacher of music, and frequented polite society, and had engaged the affections of a young lady whose father was a foreignor, and who had demanded the reason why he did not propose marriage, and was told that he could not legally marry. I have no further knowledge of him, but suspect that he was willingly a prisoner to the rebels, and was their paid spy.

I find a letter to my wife, of February 4th, informing her that I had got back to Bridgeport safely with my money. I hastened to pay it out to all entitled to it, and, knowing that I would soon be relieved, and assigned to duty as chief quartermaster of the Twentieth Corps, I issued the following order at Bridgeport.

"Circular — Captain Henry Howland A.Q.M. having been assigned to this post as senior quartermaster thereof, relieves me of my duties as quartermaster in charge. You will therefore receive orders from him from and after this date.

"My thanks are due, and are tendered to the assistant quartermasters at this post, for the constant, energetic, and faithful discharge of the very arduous and difficult as well as responsible duties imposed on them during the last three months. I desire, in particular, to express my high appreciation of the energetic and unremitting exertions of Captain T. R. Dudley, whose labors have been extraordinary, as his services have been invaluable; and the thanks of the officers of this department, at this place, to Lieutenant Colonel Huntoon, and his Michigan Engineers, for the speedy erection of the necessary buildings. It is to be regretted that the want of sawmills until quite recently caused them to labor under great disadvantages. Our thanks are also due to Major Corbin for the constant and faithful details of his thoroughly disciplined colored troops, whose services have been everywhere in demand. I desire to express my personal obligation to Lieutenant Church, of the 154th New York Vols. for the very faithful and able manner in which he has constructed the railroad side track, and superintended the details of labor elsewhere.

"We may congratulate ourselves, (well knowing as quartermasters, that we may expect congratulations from no other source,) upon the fact that, with a wretched and worn out land transportation of one hundred and one teams, with an average of three hundred and fifty employees, and an average of two hundred per day of detailed men, all of the supplies for the troops in front, sent from Nashville, have been transferred from the narrow Bridgeport platform to the steamboat landing, and reshipped to the front without delay; that we have built and equipped two steamboats, decked and equipped one hull, and repaired two old rebel vessels, and have two other vessels — steamers — partly completed; that we have cleared off the heavy forest on the river bank, and made a practical steamboat landing; that we have built a substantial side-track, with switches, one and a half miles long; two transfer depots five hundred and three hundred feet long respectively, by fifty feet wide; two warehouses, partially completed, each three hundred feet long by fifty feet wide; have put in operation four sawmills, and have another nearly ready to run, and have erected four large shops for the repairing of wagons, harness, the shoeing of mules, and other necessary work. And all this work has been done at the most unpropitious season of the year, and with insufficient help and subject to long delays for want of railroad iron, and sawmills. I tender you all my most hearty thanks, and hope we may have additional opportunity to do good service to the government we serve.

"Respectfully, W. G. LeDuc, A.Q.M.
in charge of Bridgeport."

To Captains T. R. Dudley, Arthur Edwards, J. W. Clark, D. Y. Kilgore.

XV

With General Hooker

The 11th and 12th Corps united to make the Twentieth Corps, under command of General Hooker, and my assignment to this corps was particularly agreeable to me, as I had a great admiration for General Hooker, as an experienced and able soldier, and a gentleman of wide experience and knowledge. His staff were all admirable with one exception; he soon got in a more congenial atmosphere with General Howard, with whom he had served in the 11th Corps, in Virginia; he had inherited him from Sigel, and he, I think, from Blenker. How he had ever obtained the rank of Lieutenant Colonel I do not know. He being eliminated, the staff consisted of General Daniel Butterfield, Chief of Staff; Captain H. W. Perkins, Adjutant General; Colonel James B. Fessenden; Major W. H. Lawrence; Captain R. H. Hall, Tenth Infantry, and Captain Samuel L. Taylor, of the 26th Pennsylvania Volunteers. Aides-de-camp: Lt. Col. W. G. LeDuc, Chief Quartermaster, Lt. Col. G. W. Ballock, Chief Commissary; Major Joseph R. Reynolds, Chief of Artillery; Surgeon A. H. Thurston, Medical Director; Surgeon W. O. Bennet, Medical Inspector; Captain W. E. Schofield, 82nd Ohio Volunteers, Provost Marshall; Captain J. W. Rowe, 33rd Massachusetts Volunteers, Chief of Ambulance.

We all commenced to get ready for the Atlanta campaign as we lay under the shadow of Lookout Mountain, waiting only for such an accumulation of supplies to be stored at Chattanooga as to warrant a departure from that position in pursuit of Joe Johnston. While waiting marching orders we put in the time as best we could, interspersing some amusement with our labor and drills — talk of other days and other experiences in the Army of the Potomac and elsewhere. On one occasion General Hooker was in my tent, and the conversation was about the Chancellorsville campaign. It was so interesting that after he had gone I wrote the substance of it to my wife. I will insert here a portion of a letter I wrote in 1908, (containing the substance of that letter and more), to the editor of the National Tribune, who, writing a history of the war, needed to be better informed in regard to General Hooker, and some other matters, in which people who were present could give more truthful relation than it is possible to obtain from hearsay.

"Editor National Tribune, Washington, D. C.

"The statement you make in the Tribune of date May 21st, 1908, that 'the confidence of his' (Hooker's) 'own army had been irretrievably lost at Chancellorsville', and which you doubtless intend to publish in more permanent book form, to be read and quoted and believed as truthful history, is as far from the truth as darkness is from light, and should not be allowed to stand without protest by those who know the truth. Disregard Halleck, and any other unfriend, or Halleck's clerk, Benjamin, and ask the soldiers who served in that campaign, many of whom are yet living, if they then or ever lost confidence in General Hooker. Ask the men who clambered over the rugged sides of Lookout Mountain; or those who, on the firing line, were driving the enemy through the open woods near Hope Church, Georgia, when they heard the cheering close behind them, and turned and saw "Old Joe" and a single staff officer trying to cheer in that din of battle, and who took it up — the whole line for a mile or more took it up — and drowned the firing with their huzzas; or ask any of the Twentieth Corps men, who, with sorrowful faces and moistened eyes bade him farewell when, under the walls of Atlanta, he resented the indignity put upon him by General Sherman, who appointed Howard to the place left vacant by the death of McPherson, which of right belonged to Hooker, who promptly demanded to be relieved from serving with Sherman. Don't go to a bureau clerk in Washington to find out if we, who served at the front, ever lost confidence in Hooker. His order when we returned to our old camps from Chancellorsville expressed the feelings of the army then, and don't you write otherwise if you would write truthful history.

"I was in the army of the Potomac when that inexcusable, blundering attack ordered by Burnside was made; and when the foolish attempt to march through the bottomless mud of Virginia was made; and then saw, with distress, the disorganized army melting away like ice under the midsummer sun, by desertion. (There was seen want of confidence in the general in command, and in the administration that had selected such a commander.) I saw it reorganized, and drilled and disciplined by Generals Hooker and Butterfield until confidence was restored and never lost again by any soldiers under the command of General Joseph Hooker. The men behind the guns felt that they would never be required to try such experimental slaughter as that required by General Sherman at Kenesaw, or the deliberate butchery required by General Grant in the Wilderness. Instead of loss of confidence, confidence was firmly established in the minds of those who participated in the brilliant strategy of that campaign of Chancellorsville. A commander had at last been found who could not only organize an army, but could skillfully march and fight it, or refuse battle when the interests of the country required it.

"When, by discipline, he had brought the army into condition for service he sought an opening for employment, and to give further instruction in marching and fighting. His plans being well considered were made known to no one but his chief of staff, who was enjoined to secrecy. By his numerous spies he was well informed. One of them had dined at the table with Jefferson Davis. Another had measured the water on Germania Ford, on the Rapidan, and one reported the number of rations issued to the rebel army the day before the advance of the 11th Corps. Thus he knew all about the rebel army, and where it was.

"His intention was to take Richmond, whether, in taking it, he whipped Lee or not. The 11th and 12th corps were at Stafford, in the rear of the main army. Their movements could not be seen, or their absence noticed by the enemy, and they were ordered to march early in the morning, with the 11th in advance, and to make Kelly's Ferry as soon as possible. Orders would reach them at that place. The orders there received were waiting for them, and were to cross immediately, and push for Germania Ford on the Rapidan. So speedy was this march that they surprised the rebel forces on the Rapidan building a bridge across the river. The advance of the 11th Corps crossed the stream — water breast high — and captured all the bridge builders who did not run away. Both the 11th and 12th Corps crossed the river that night — the third night out. This gave control of the United States Ford at the mouth of the Rapidan, and a pontoon bridge was thrown across over which passed all the other troops designed to cross above Fredericksburg. Meanwhile Sedgewick threw a pontoon bridge across below, and was ordered to cross and drive the enemy out of the town, and the next day occupy the heights. Position was taken at Chancellorsville, and the attack which Lee was forced to make was awaited and desired. He attacked in front, as expected, and was repulsed. Then Jackson made his flank movement on our right, and found the Eleventh Corps wholly unprepared for defence, and he rolled them back on the main body of the army. This necessitated the taking up, during the night, of a new position, which the enemy attacked the next morning, when they suffered a bitter repulse.

"Sedgewick, excellent soldier that he was, had taken Fredericksburg, but failed to come to time as ordered. He was too late to fill the place at which he was to be at daylight, but toward which he did not attempt to move until after nine o'clock in the morning. After nine he had to fight for what he could have walked peacefully over before. That night found Sedgewick at Bank's Ferry, and Hooker's fine strategic operations nullified. He was now in a position where he could not profit by his superior forces; where he could only use the heads of columns, and where Lee could bring as many men into action as Hooker could; where tactics and strategy would amount to nothing, and where his soldiers must be subjected simply to the necessity of a murderous contest in which the side that could suffer the most and have a few men left would be victorious, and then with the possibility that his army would be so weakened as to be incapable of taking advantage of a victory thus won. Hooker then determined to try another scheme. He telegraphed Sedgewick asking if he could hold Bank's Ferry until morning. Sedgewick telegraphed that he could not, and half an hour later that he could, which last telegram was delayed on the way an hour or more — too late for the move Hooker had in mind. This was to cross to the east side, at United States Ford, then march down and cross at Bank's Ferry, join Sedgewick and march for Richmond direct on the shortest line, and on the best roads. Lee would have been on his right, where Hooker had maneuvered to get him, without supplies, and on a difficult road. Hooker's teams were all loaded with ten days supplies and were kept ready to start at word of command. A million rations were on ship board awaiting his order to meet him at the Pamunky, or at the White House, or wherever ordered.

"General Hooker's magnificent strategic attempt to take Richmond failed through the failure, first of Stoneman, who did nothing that he should have done; then of Howard, who neglected to obey a positive order to put the Eleventh Corps in a proper position to repel attack; and of Sedgewick — good soldier — who failed to be on time at the place where he was ordered to be, and finally of the telegraphic service which failed to deliver a telegram. What a succession of adversities tending to defeat the splendid strategy of the campaign! The most inexcusable was the neglect of Howard to promptly obey the order which he says in an article printed and published in the Century 'neither reached me nor, to my knowledge, my adjutant Colonel Mysenberg', but which General Schurz says in McClure's Magazine, June 1907, page 166, he, Schurz, 'read and delivered to him that identical dispatch, which was followed by another animated discussion between us in which I most earnestly, but without effect, endeavored to convince him that in case of such an attack from the west our right, as then posted, would be hopelessly overwhelmed.' This order was as follows:

"Headquarters of the Army of the Potomac, Chancellorsville, May 2nd, 1863, 9:30 A.M. Major Generals Slocum and Howard: I am directed by the Major General commanding to say that the disposition you have made of your corps has been with a view to a front attack by the enemy. If he should throw himself upon your flank he wishes you to examine the ground and determine the position you will take in that event in order that you may be prepared for him in whatever direction he advances. He suggests that you have heavy reserves well in hand to meet this contingency. The right of your line does not appear to him to be strong enough. No artificial defences worth naming appear to have been thrown up — not in the General's opinion as favorable as might be. Please advance your pickets as far as may be safe in order to obtain timely notice of their approach. J. H. Van Allen, Brig. Gen. and aide-de-camp."

Colonel Mysenburg is dead, but as contributary to an understanding of this question it is well to include here an extract from

a letter from N. M. Kellog — to me well known during his long
and honorable service in the Eleventh Corps as a man of probity
and intelligence, — whose intimate acquaintance with the facts
entitles him to be heard and to be believed. This is what he says:
"I was in the adjutant general's office under Lieutenant Colonel
Mysenburg at Howard's headquarters during the Chancellorsville
and Gettysburg campaigns; while there I had charge of the letters
and telegrams received. The famous 9:30 A.M. May 2nd, 1863 order of Hooker's to Slocum and Howard in the field at Chancellorsville was received and was kept from the files until two months
afterward, and twenty-four hours after 'old Joe' was relieved was
then slipped into my hand to be recorded and filed, at Emmets-
burg, Maryland, June 30th, after all danger of Howard's court
martial was over."

Hooker was a general fitted by education, by experience, and by
the highest qualities of mind and heart, to command men in the
great game of war — not playing the game to kill men — not even
his enemies, unless by their sacrifice the cause of his country could
be advanced or sustained. His sobriquet of "Fighting Joe," the
catch word of some correspondent of the newspaper fraternity,
annoyed him always, as by it he had the reputation of being an
irascible, impulsive bruiser. The name was misleading, and has
caused a misapprehension of his character and motives, especially
to those who have attempted to explain Chancellorsville. Commanding as he did an army largely outnumbering the rebel army
he had so brilliantly surprised, but ignorant of the wilderness in
which he found himself confronted by Lee — fortified by the forest
almost as impregnably as he was at Marye's Heights when attacked by Burnside — these critics cannot understand why the
"Fighting Joe" of their imagination did not pitch in, kill and be
killed, until he had worn out Lee's army. Then that would be the
end of their thinking. They would let the future take care of
itself. Even the intellectual Carl Schurz, who was very much per
sonally present at Chancellorsville, cannot understand why Hooker seemed to lose his aggressiveness and wait for Lee to attack him.
Schurz was not in command of the army with all the responsibility
such command entailed. Hooker was, and realized that he was
entrusted with the lives of a hundred and thirty thousand men
with whom to help put down the rebellion — not simply to con-
quer the rebel army of Virginia. He had been advised by the Presi-

dent that the political condition of the country and the shock of the unnecessary loss of life at Fredericksburg by Burnside was such that probably another army could not be raised, and that therefore he must be careful to avoid any great risk. He had his army where he invited and desired an attack by Lee, who, having once tried, declined to make another assault. For Hooker to advance in the Wilderness was to fight only by the heads of columns, where his superiority in numbers would avail him little. He would win in the murderous contest, but it would put the country in mourning, and would it end the war? Certainly not at that time. The administration was anxious to have an advance and a victory. Chancellorsville was a victory for the Union whatever may be said of the rolling up of the Eleventh Corps. No troops could or would or should have stood if placed as they were, and surprised and assaulted by three times their number. Their disaster was temporary. The final victory was with the army of the Potomac, but it was an incomplete victory, and Hooker knew he would be blamed for not following it up at whatever cost. It was for him to determine whether he would sacrifice the lives of many men to win glory for himself, and a not sufficient advantage for the country. Well might he take time to consider while waiting for and inviting Lee to attack.

Schurz could not understand his inaction. It has been suggested that he had had too much whiskey or that he was suffering from the want of it and afraid to trust himself with a canteen, and other such foolish twaddle and idle thoughtless gabble is offered in explanation of what explains itself. Hooker, knowing that he could whip Lee, knowing too that it would gain him great applause and credit, knew also that the enemy, having advantage of position, would make it cost him dear, and that it would not end the war at that time; that the capture of the rebel capital would do more at that time than winning a battle over Lee's army. He knew that Lee would not attack; and that Sedgewick could not hold on till morning while Hooker made a night march and joined him, and thus forced Lee to emerge. He sacrificed his own ambition, and wisely and safely brought his army back to their old camps, and continued their discipline and drill until the time came to check Lee in his every move and meet him at Gettysburg. This was all done under Hooker's orders, although Meade had the credit of winning that battle.

As I have often said, and as everyone who was in Hooker's army from Fredericksburg to Gettysburg said, had Hooker been in command after Gettysburg, Lee's army would never have crossed the Potomac except as prisoners. Meade might have captured Lee, but he would not. Lee had to make pontoons out of torn down houses. The river was in freshet and very rapid. He expected to have to fight, and had not sufficient ammunition for a battle, and no source of supply. He expected an attempt to capture him, and dreaded the result, and rushed the making of pontoons. Meade's army lay encamped around him, eager to attack and make an end of the rebellion then and there. Meade said he was waiting to get ready. Apparently he was waiting for Lee to cross; and might have loaned him pontoons if he had applied for them. Meade was an engineer of the regular army. Engineers never attack unless compelled. They are strong on the defensive.

In a conversation with Hooker in his log hut under the shadow of Lookout Mountain (after the capture of that mountain under Hooker's personal direction,) he suddenly stopped in his walk up and down the dirt floor, and said seriously and reverently: "Le Duc, it was much more difficult to bring myself to give that order to recross the river than you can imagine; the country expected an advance, and I could have made an advance and whipped the enemy, and I knew it; but it would have put the country in sackcloth and ashes; I knew that too. And I also knew that it would not end the war at that time. No, I think it was providential that I brought that army back safe and sound and in good condition for the march to and victory at Gettysburg. Don't you think so?" I did think so then, only a few months after Gettysburg, and I am certain of it now, forty five years after. A French historian suggests that possibly Hooker's accident on the porch, that laid him senseless for an hour or more, might have been the cause of his inaction at Chancellorsville. The blow was on the side of the body and the leg, and did not affect the brain, although after the war his right side was paralyzed.

General Hooker and General Butterfield were talking over the capture of Lookout Mountain one day in my hearing, while in camp at Wauhatchie, and General Hooker said: "When Geary was up on the mountain side he sent me word that if the clouds lifted and disclosed his position he did not think he could hold it. I sent him word to push ahead, and before the clouds lifted we would come down in the valley, cross over, and help him; this we did, and thus captured the rebel troops that held the works on the side of the mountain, and before the clouds lifted we had the position and prisoners all safe. The next day when we rushed across the mountain side and started to Rossville, we were delayed at Chattanooga Creek to make a bridge, and the enemy destroyed another bridge beyond Rossville which delayed us some hours. On the second day if Grant had only made a noise on the left to keep them there, and thrown every available man forward toward Ringold, they would have been caught like quails in a trap."

Butterfield said: "If Thomas' staff had only had the proper snap in them we would have captured six thousand more prisoners than we did. It was with difficulty, and only after persistent talk that I got the pontoons ordered out, and then you know the officer left them at Rossville and came forward himself, and thus we had a long delay at the creek, and could not get the artillery across. Do you remember, General, when we were near Ringold there was a long halt of Palmer's troops, and we rode forward to see what the trouble was? I was behind when we passed through Osterause's troops, and I heard one soldier say to another: 'There now — there goes old Fighting Joe — and you may as well look to your kit and get ready to go forward. Somebody will know what to do now, instead of squatting around all day!' " . . .

XVI

On to Atlanta

When General Sherman began preparations for the advance toward Atlanta he sent for an old acquaintance whom he had known in the regular army, and who had been post quartermaster at Fort Leavenworth for many years, and had been apparently forgotten. Sherman made him chief quartermaster. Having seen no service with armies in the field he was a failure to begin with, and was too old to learn quickly. He started out with rules and regulations he had found comfortable in the fort, closed his office at four o'clock, and would see no one on business before nine in the morning. This was absurd in an army in active service, where quartermasters must be in readiness at all hours of the day or night. He expected clothing, shoes, and the like to last a certain time, according to regulations, and if they did not the soldier was to blame, and must do without. In making up transportation for the expected movement southward he limited everything to the least possible, and made no provision for marching. Colonel McKay and I decided that we would not confine our supplies to his limits, but would provide enough to secure the efficiency of our troops on the march through the rough, mountainous country, reporting enough to comply with orders, and holding a reserve where we could readily make it useful. I knew the gravel of the southern mountains had not been ground smooth by the glaciers of the ice period, and the sharp angles would cut the contract-made shoes of the soldiers, and the feet of the mules and horses. I took sixty or seventy extra wagons loaded with supplies of all kinds, and I had a drove of three hundred mules in the by ways, out of sight, usually for the relief of broken down animals.

Hayes, chief quartermaster of Howard's corps, had less experience, and obeyed orders implicitly, with the result that, after a week's marching and fighting, it was necessary to send back to Chattanooga for supplies for the 14th corps, and this caused a halt of the army. Hayes was a faithful, hard working officer, and did all that could be done with the means at command; but Howard's corps could not move on time as ordered for want of transportation.

General Sherman having ordered the seizure of the engines and cars from railroads north of the Ohio river, the quartermaster's department was able to accumulate sufficient quantity of supplies to warrant the forward movement of the army against the position of the rebels at Dalton, where the rebel general, Joe Johnston, was entrenched in a position which seemed impregnable. It is not my purpose to give a history of the campaign or operation of the armies. All that can be had from histories written by others. I only mention such incidents personal to myself as I think will be of interest to you and others of our family and friends.

I give an extract here from a letter to my wife.

"May 15th. My tent was pitched in Snake Creek Gap late in the evening, and being very tired I lay down to rest, but was soon disturbed by the muffled crying or sobbing of a little babe, and I rose and went to a little house near by around which was the débris of a battle fought the day before by McPherson's men. The garden fence had been broken down, and all around was the disorder of a battle field. The house was a log cabin, weather boarded, a building with one room and with a window — that is a square hole in one end, with a shutter hung on hinges on the outside — no sash or frame for glazing. As the cry seemed to come from the house I went to the window, and looked in. There was but one bed, occupied, as was the floor, with wounded or sick men who were being ministered to by a little woman who was making some preparation of food or medicine by an open fire, assisted by a soldier. Two little scared looking children, six or eight years old, were standing near the window. As soon as she had done waiting on some one of the wounded she approached the window, and asked: 'Is there anything I can do for you?' I said: 'No, Madam, is there anything I can do to relieve the little babe I hear crying occasionally?' 'But there is no babe crying,' she said, 'I have no baby — only these two children.' 'I certainly heard the plaintive cry of a child — there — don't you hear it?' 'Oh, that' she answered, 'is the bleat of my boy's little pet lamb; he hid it under a box in the shed when the others of our flock were killed.' 'And is this all you have left you?' 'Yes, sir; our stock is all gone; our cows, sheep, hogs, chickens, and bacon and meal — all but a little put up in the loft overhead.' As the brave little woman told her story she did not cry, but every tone of her voice was a tear.

"I asked my orderly if he couldn't get some water for the little boy's lamb; he said he would like to do it. And I told Felch to give her two sacks of corn. She can live on parched corn for a time, until she can look around. He said: 'Yes, sir; thank you for the chance.' I told him to put it away somewhere, so that it wouldn't be taken away from her. I will go myself, and see what place she has for it.

"I have just come from her house. The little lamb is fed and has ceased it's plaintive bleating. Mrs. ———— has her corn, also some pork. Her tearful voice followed me: 'I am — very much obliged to you, sir.' If I don't write as well as usual it is because I do not see quite clearly."

We did not have orders to march early in the morning as I had expected, and I saw more of Mrs. ————, and her faithful nursing of our wounded, and gave her a note to be delivered to the surgeon of a hospital which was a short distance in the rear, recommending her to his protection and assistance.

Another paragraph in this letter to my wife say: "Mrs. ————'s husband is a lieutenant in the rebel army, and she says she thinks he will come home now if he can get away. He said he would not retreat beyond his home. But she says if he or anyone says anything like that they would be arrested, and perhaps shot; that he has many enemies in the rebel army, and she fears he may not be able to get away. The people of Georgia are divided in opinion as to the confederacy. All northern Georgia was opposed to secession, and evidently she is of a family who were opposed."

The great campaign for the capture of Atlanta — one of the most memorable in history — occupied four months of the year 1864, and was conducted by two of the greatest military men of the day, General William T. Sherman on the union side, and General Joseph Johnston on the rebel side. Sherman, with twice the men Johnston had, moved to attack him where he lay awaiting and desiring an attack behind his fortifications at Dalton. An examination of these defences convinced Sherman of the folly of making an attack. He commenced a series of flank operations which were continued to the end of the campaign with but one unfortunate exception, that of the attack on Kenesaw. At the very outset both commanders blundered. Sherman sent McPherson through Snake Creek Gap to cut off the retreat of Johnston's army along the railroad, and thus cut off his means of supply. McPherson went through the Gap, but did not throw his force across the railroad. When Hooker, whose command was following McPherson's, saw his error, and that only by intervening between Resaca and Dalton could the enemy be driven from his line of retreat, offered through General Thomas to do the work, asking to be allowed to throw his corps across the line of railroad between Dalton and Resaca, Sherman denied the request for the reason — as I believe — that he would not give Hooker an opportunity to gain the credit that his favorite, McPherson, had failed to secure.

Sherman and Hooker had quarreled in their younger days in California, and with Sherman the fire was never extinguished; the old animosity remained, and prevented harmonious action between these two very able officers. I once had an opportunity to relieve their embarrassment. At the battle of Hope Church, after Hooker had driven the enemy a mile or more, there was a lull in the firing in which the men were replenishing their ammunition, and were eating. I had occasion to see General Hooker, and found him with General Sherman, sitting at a table of some kind on which lunch had been served. As I came up I noticed that they had finished eating, and that they had remained sitting when the fire broke out afresh, neither wishing to rise first. I said: "It looks to me as if one school boy was afraid, and the other 'dassent'." They both laughed, rose, and together moved away. A moment after they rose a ball smashed the arm of the chair in which Hooker had been sitting. I had it repaired, and it now serves useful purposes here at home.

Johnston never again offered the like opportunity to Sherman to cut his line of supply that he did by a tardy retreat from Dalton. He resisted Sherman's advance, but always retreated in time to save his line of communications, and to find other defensive works prepared in his rear. The wise Fabian policy of Johnston was not approved by the rebel president, and he deposed him and appointed Hood to command the rebel forces. This was very gratifying to Sherman, for Hood's aggressive tactics were what Sherman desired. Hood was severely punished in two desperate attacks, and remained behind his fortifications in Atlanta. Sherman, finding his cavalry raids in Hood's rear ineffectual, placed the Twentieth Corps to hold the great bridge across the Chattahoochie, and, with the remainder of the army, made a grand détour around the city, destroying Hood's lines of communication with his sources of supply. This brought Hood out of the city in a hurry, after destroying by fire all he could not carry, which was little beside the food carried by the soldiers. General Slocum, with a detachment of the Twentieth, entered the city on one side as the rebels left it on the other, on September 2nd.

I happened to be at the telegraph station when notice came from General Slocum that he was in possession of the city, together with orders to move up the corps, the transportation, and all except a bridge guard. I immediately sent a message to General Meigs at Washington, and one to my wife at Mt. Vernon, Ohio, saying: "Atlanta is captured and we are in possession of the city", which she received September 3rd, in the morning. The wires were cut directly after my messages had passed, and it was several days before General Sherman could communicate and assure the President of the fact. At Mt. Vernon, Knox County, Ohio, a political convention was in progress, the Copperheads were shouting that the war was a failure; that Atlanta could not be taken. My wife took her message to a prominent Union man, and asked him to read it to the convention. He hastened to interrupt a speaker, and asked the attention of the people while he read a telegram. The effect was electrical. The convention dissolved in a celebration by the Unionists. The capture of Atlanta had a very beneficial effect on the election then pending.

I went into the city, and took a room in the house of Judge Lyon. It was a large brick house, on a corner. A door in the middle gave entrance to a wide hall. On the left was a reception room, and on the right a large double parlor. I set up my desk in the reception room, and was busy with my work until after nine o'clock. Hearing some piano playing and singing in the parlor, I stepped across the hall and stood by the open door listening to the music made by a little lady, dressed in black, seated at the piano. She commenced to sing "Maryland, my Maryland." A little child was standing in the doorway, and I said to her in a low voice, "Go and tell that lady she must not sing that song tonight." The little girl stepped to the piano, and delivered the message, and the lady arose, and said, angrily, "I did not wish to sing it — your officers here insisted upon it!" There were several officers present. I said: "Gentlemen, you should have been more thoughtful. You know our troops are marching by this place, and, hearing a song like that, might throw a missile through the window endangering that lady's life." The music was ended. The officers departed, and the night was restful.

In the morning very early I was writing at my desk when I heard a sudden screaming in the hall, and on opening the door I saw the lady pianist throwing her arms wildly about, and crying: "They have taken my boy away from me!"

An old gray haired man was standing in the hall, and of him I inquired what he had been telling her. "When Hood's body guard left the city yesterday they took her boy with them," he said. "They made him drunk, and carried him off!"

"How do you know this?"

"He and I were in the same company in the trenches."

"Were you enlisted?"

"No, but I was compelled to take a musket in defense of the city, and so was the boy."

"How old are you?"

"Eighty two."

"And the boy?"

"Fourteen, I was told."

Hood had robbed the cradle and the grave to fill his trenches. I told the mother Hood's people would have no use for the boy, and when he got sober he would come back to the city, and our pickets would take him in hand, and I would see that he was returned to her. (This happened.) She became quiet, and I went back to my work. . . .

I had a very busy, troublesome task in turning the people of Atlanta out of the city. A neutral camp was established about twelve miles from the city to which were sent all those wishing to go south. To this place people were permitted to take with them all such articles as were not contraband, as were fire arms, and the like. The order was sent to me by Charles Ewing, Sherman's brother-in-law, serving on his staff at that time, I think with the rank of Lieutenant Colonel. When I read it I said: "Charley, tell

Cump Sherman from me that this order won't read well in history."

"All right," he answered, "I'll tell him, but it won't make any difference."

"I know that, but I want him to know how others look at it."

I saw Ewing again in the afternoon. "Did you tell Cump?"

"Yes, and he said 'You tell Bill Duc I care not a damn how others read it — I am making the history, and the citizens of this rebel town shan't eat the rations I need for my army. Tell him to turn them out.'"

I changed my quarters to Richard Peters' place, and had a large yard, and a long walk from the gate to the porch where my table and papers were. The people came here to get their orders for the transportation of whatever they desired and were permitted to take out, and to learn whether it was to be taken by rail or wagon. The mayor of the city was enlisted to help his people, and was very useful in promoting their comfort and quiet obedience to orders. James M. Calhoun was a better adviser for his countrymen than his distinguished relative John C.; and at the end of the truce and of the migration he sent a letter of thanks to those engaged in transfering the citizens and their property out of the city. . . .

At the neutral ground we established a cooking outfit, and provided so that no one need go away hungry, or without a cup of coffee. Occasionally I went out myself in an ambulance, and took with me some mothers and their children. Mr. and Mrs. Markham were desirous of sending their daughter Mrs. Robert Lowry and her husband out of the confederacy to remain until the war was ended, and as I was going on my leave of absence of thirty days they asked if they might accompany me. To this I assented, and in my preparation for the journey provided for them. I was taking some of my camp equipage, and two horses I wished to send home. I had also a cook and a hostler, and it was necessary to take food for there were no passenger trains, and no passenger cars and no regular time table. We might be on the road a week or two weeks.

One of my two horses I had brought from Virginia, and had ridden through the Gettysburg campaign. I bought him from a German officer whose father in Germany had died, and the son had succeeded to the chieftaincy of the family, and resigned from the Army of the Potomac. I bought his horse, a handsome thoroughbred of possum gray color. Some time previous an Indiana cavalry-man whose term of enlistment had expired, and who owned his horse, came to me wishing me to buy him for the army. This I declined to do, but if he would trade his serviceable horse to the government for a colt that had been captured near Calhoun I would buy the colt from him. This he had done, and I wished to take my two army horses and the colt home. I had had a car fitted up for the horses, and another for Mr. and Mrs. Lowry and myself, with plenty of straw in the bottom, a curtain across, and a bed made on the floor of the car for them. They were as comfortable as could be expected until we could reach passenger-car accomoda-tions. I had some business with the provost marshall before start-ing, and went to his office. Here I found him in dispute with an irate surgeon, who was declaiming when I went in about a pris-oner recently captured whose wife had been a nurse under the sur-geon at Snake Creek Gap. I asked how it came about that a rebel woman was a nurse in our hospital. The surgeon said she had come to him with a letter of recommendation from a union office; and here was the letter. I took it, and it was my letter given to Mrs. ——— at Snake Creek Gap. I told the provost that the man was a willing prisoner; a deserter I did not doubt, in fact, as his wife had told me he had promised to desert if the rebel army retreated beyond his place at the Gap. If he could get safely north he would never be in the rebel army again, as he was there by com-pulsion. And I urged him to let his wife take him, and give him transportation to the north.

Many years after the war when these things were a hidden mem-ory, I received a letter from Mrs. ———, from Kansas. My brother, Doctor Harry Le Duc, had been a member of the legislature and, seeing his name, she had found my address. She and her husband had come north, settled in Kansas on a homestead, and were pros-pering with a family of children. I helped to get for her a place on the union pension roll for nurses.

When I arrived at Nashville with the Lowrys we abandoned the freight train, sent it on, and went to a hotel for the night, and the next morning took the regular passenger train for Louisville, and, when we got into the highlands of Kentucky, found our freight train had been captured by Ferguson's guerillas. My horses, stores, and servants had been run off into the retreat of that band. I had a letter some time afterward from one of my servants who could write, and who had been paid his wages in a check which I was enabled to save him. They had been robbed of everything. He reported that there was great rejoicing over the capture of my horses, and that they at once got up some races, in which my possum gray easily beat everything. It was a satisfaction to learn, after a time, that Ferguson and several of his gang had been captured and hanged.

The Lowrys got safely through to New York by way of Canada, where they deposited a portion of the thirty thousand dollars in gold they had brought through with me on the freight car. I was told — by whom I do not remember — nor do I know if it was true — that Lowry speculated in Wall Street with the balance of the gold, bidding against the government, and lost it all. However that may have been, he is today a very prosperous banker in Atlanta — indeed well known all over the United States — and a much respected citizen. . . .

XVII

The Beginning of the End

Coming north on my leave of absence I went first to Mt. Vernon, Ohio, to see my wife and children, and then to Minnesota to look after a house the building of which had been contracted for before I entered the army, and to pick up some loose ends of business and to relieve as much as possible my brother, a Presbyterian minister, from his care of my farms and other interests which he had faithfully looked after during my absence; and also to electioneer for the re-election of Lincoln. For this I got an extension of my leave of absence of thirty days, toward the close of which I returned to Mt. Vernon, and from there to Cincinnatti to take a boat to Louisville, and then by rail to my command at Atlanta. . . .

Returning now to my army history in 1865: A few days before my leave of absence expired, I found myself in Nashville, and reported to General Thomas, who, on seeing me exclaimed: "The very man I want. You cannot join your command, for General Sherman has cut communications, and is now leaving Atlanta. My quartermaster, McKay, is in Chattanooga, and Schofield is in trouble with his transportation, and I want you to take a place on my staff as chief quartermaster in the field, and go down to meet Schofield as soon as possible." I thanked the General, and accepted the task with pleasure, and set about getting a horse, and the equipment necessary. I started as soon as possible and, arriving at Franklin, made preparations for the crossing of the transportation over the Harpeth River, planking the railroad bridge, and selecting a place for the parking of the trains half a mile back from the river. I slept on the porch of a house not far from the road, and about two o'clock in the morning was wakened by the advance of the wagon train, which I had placed in park, and then rode across to meet General Schofield in Franklin. I found him and his staff officers at the house of a Doctor ——, standing around a table eating, and drinking hot coffee served by the mistress of the house and her servants. A more tired and sleepy looking party there was not. I noted that they would take a few winks of sleep while drinking the coffee, or eating what they could gather from the table.

I reported the transportation parked across the river, and expected to see the troops marching over the bridge to take station on the Nashville side; but they were placed around the town, as if to protect it from assault by the rebels. I think, however, that General Schofield was so worn out and sleepy that he did not understand the situation, but thought he must protect his transportation while crossing the river. Hood saw his error, and hastened to charge the thin line before the soldiers could be marched across the river. He is said to have told his men: "Break the line, and I will take you to the Ohio River."

I had personally seen to it that everything on wheels was across the river before noon except an ammunition train for artillery, which was held in readiness to move at a moment's notice. About the middle of the afternoon I was with Generals Schofield and Wilson, in a fortification on the Nashville side of the river; Wilson was reporting that Forrest's cavalry had crossed the river, and were heading toward Murfreesboro, or intending to turn and interpose between him and Nashville. I said: "Then it is important that we have some troops at the pass through the hills. If he gets possession of that pass he will capture all our trains; a single regiment or less can defend it against cavalry, for I noticed long ranks of cord wood at the pass that can be used for defense." I asked that a detachment of cavalry be sent to hold the place, until a regiment of infantry could be marched to take possession. Wilson said his entire command was fending off in that direction, and he thought Forrest was going to Murfreesboro hoping to surprise them there.

General Wilson rode off, as I understood to check any move of Forrest's in the direction of Brentwood Pass. I asked General Schofield if I should start the trains, as the animals had been fed and watered, and were ready to move. He said: "Not yet; it might encourage the enemy. Better wait till dark."

About this time the enemy were preparing for the assault. As the firing became rapid General Stanley, who was with Schofield on the north side of the river, galloped across to join his troops and take a very active part in driving back the enemy who had crossed our little breast-work thrown up by our men with their hands and bayonets, mostly a light bank hardly a foot high, behind which they lay and fired deadly volleys into the charging rebels, who had to approach without any cover over a quarter of a mile of open ground. The assault was pushed with determination to break through, and they did at one place, but were finally driven back, and left their dead inside our lines. Pat Cleburne, their bravest general, lay with his horse across the little bank of earth that marked the line of resistance. Hood's loss was terrible, and his men would not try again. Schofield gathered up his wounded, and during the night retreated to Nashville. The battle of Franklin took all of the fight out of Hood's army. They never made another determined stand except at Overton Hill, from which they were driven by Negroes.

General Schofield took a great and unnecessary risk in holding the position around Franklin when he might have put the river between his army and the enemy. He thought he was protecting the crossing of his transportation, as he afterward explained, but his transportation was all across before one o'clock, noon. I had occasion to apply to Schofield's chief quartermaster, Colonel Hiram Hayes, for confirmation of this statement, and in reply he sent me a statement of the troubles and anxieties he, as quartermaster of Schofield's trains on the retreat, had had from Pulaski; and, in the following letter of date August 8, 1904, settles the matter.

"I came to the bridge over the Harpeth River early in the morning of the thirtieth of November, 1864, and found the trains passing over the railroad bridge which had been planked for the purpose. The transportation was on the north side, and was over by the hour I have indicated, viz., one o'clock P.M. We had been in a row all night, never knowing where war (Hell) would break out from below — that is from the line of retreat on which we had been crowding all sail so as to avoid a premature encounter with Hood. When I got to the bridge and saw the property moving across to comparative safety for the moment, I felt thankful beyond expression. We did cross by noon of the thirtieth, or very nearly.

My transportation did not get on to the bridge before the morning of the thirtieth. I know this, for we did not start from Spring Hill until about one A.M. The army trains were all piled into Franklin together in the morning of November thirtieth. Another thing is true. The trains did not delay the troops from any lack of their moving just as fast and a little faster than the exigencies would permit. Everybody took mighty good care to keep his place in the movement and accelerate his motion. I have tried to study General Schofield's account which is very minute and particular. And after all is said and done it can be summed up by saying that it was the Hand of the Lord and his Right Arm that delivered us out of the hands of the enemy on the twenty-ninth and thirtieth. I never knew who fixed up that bridge until you told me in this letter that I have just received from you. But it was always a source of gratitude to the unknown benefactor who smoothed the passage of the river in that way. I have thought of this precise thing uncounted times, and the scene of the crossing that November morning of fate is as fresh in my mind as if it had occurred but yesterday."

As it turned out, the terrible repulse Hood received at Franklin was of great assistance to General Thomas in the attack he made on Hood's lines around Nashville, by which the rebel army was destroyed. General Thomas was in no hurry to attack Hood in the intrenchments he was allowed to construct around Nashville, for he was informed of the coming of desired reinforcements with which he was determined to annihilate Hood when he did strike. On the arrival of the reinforcements (A. J. Smith and his veterans), the weather turned cold and severe for the latitude of Nashville. Rain, snow, sleet and freezing nights were bad for the rebel army, unfed, unclothed, and with no suitable tent covering. Every day's delay was for their ruin. This was not understood at Washington, or at Grant's headquarters. They feared that the deliberate Thomas would allow Hood to cross the Cumberland River into Kentucky: but of that there was never the least danger at any time. Hood had reached the limit of his rash move. Thomas was ready, and would have attacked three days before he did, but for the sleet covered ground which prevented the movement of artillery and cavalry. I was with General Thomas when he rode along the right to observe the effect of the cavalry movement to turn the left of the enemy, and the succeeding charge of Smith's troops over the breastworks and up a hill, driving the enemy before them, or capturing many of them who threw down their guns and were willingly made captives to get something to eat.

There were many Minnesota boys among Smith's troops, and it was pleasant to see the way they fought up to and over the breast-works, and after the fleeing rebels. Colonels W. R. Marshall and L. F. Hubbard with their regiments made no stop at the breast works, and it was for the Johnnies to surrender or run. While riding along the lines a soldier accosted me with: "Oh, Mr. Le Duc, brother Perry is shot! Won't you see if he is dead?" "Who is brother Perry?" "Don't you remember? We used to bring you milk in St. Paul." I got off my horse to examine brother Perry, who was prudently lying behind an oak tree. I found a ball had struck his shoulder, glancing up and out without mashing the bones; a pain-ful wound, but not dangerous. "Go back to the hospital," I ad-vised him, "and have your wound dressed. In six months you would not take five hundred dollars for it." He took my advice, and, after a few months, was back in the army.

The overthrow and destruction of Hood's army at Nashville is common history. In this I took an active part in keeping the supply trains up to the pursuing troops, and as the enemy were fleeing for their lives, and Wilson's cavalry was pushing their rear, we had lively work for two weeks. On the second day of the pursuit, after we had gone through Brentwood Pass, and turned to the right toward Franklin, I was in the rear giving some directions about the repair of a bridge, when an officer approached on a gallop, his horse in a lather, and said: "You are on General Thomas' staff? Do you know if I am right in taking the pontoons out on the Murfreesboro pike? I have gone down the pike for some miles, and I fear it is a mistake."

"I think it is certainly a mistake."

"Well, here is the order. Won't you correct it?"

I looked the order over, and saw it read 'Murfreesboro pike,' and I knew that the Murfreesboro and Franklin pikes are the same until through Brentwood Pass. "The order was not issued through me," I said, "and I don't know the reason that may be behind it. You will have to ride on, and get General Thomas' correction. He is a short distance ahead." This he did, but the delay of the pontoons at Duck River cost us nearly a day, and was of great importance to the rebels, many more of whom would otherwise have fallen into our hands before we were stopped at Pulaski by the bottomless mud of the country roads. The pike, or stone road terminated at Pulaski. There is a bridge across the little river that skirts the town. A lady who lived near the bridge, and who saw the rebel army passing, told me that she saw General Hood standing on an elevated place by the roadside as the soldiers marched by, and heard them curse him awfully, and say: "You damned old fool — when are going to have another killing? The Yanks have got one of your legs — I wish they had your whole damned body."

There were a lot of muskets at Pulaski, and each soldier was given one to carry, but when they got to the bridge they threw them over into the stream. The ground, frozen when the rebel troops passed over, had thawed when we arrived, and the mud was impassible for cannon and transportation of supplies, and I so reported, after an examination, to General Thomas. He took some members of his staff and crossed the bridge and rode a short distance to be satisfied that to go farther was impossible unless the roads should freeze again — which was not probable. There the pursuit terminated. At the crossing of Duck River, before the pontoons came up, I was sounding the river and planning to make a temporary bridge in place of one the rebels had destroyed, and found some pieces of artillery, bright new brass twelve-pounder Napoleon guns. Getting a rope fastened to the carriage I passed it ashore, and the officers and men hauled on the line and brought up possibly three pieces the rebels had dumped off the bridge. I left them on the bank, and they were gathered in by some battery men I suppose.

As the rebel army was passing through Franklin in the morning after the battle, some ladies were waving their handkerchiefs as the soldiers marched by. A soldier stopped and addressed them in a serious tone of voice. "Ladies, there is a better use for your handkerchiefs out on the field where the dead and wounded lie. You have waved us into this, but you can't help us out. Put up your handkerchiefs — this is no time for waving!"

Soon after we returned to Nashville I received orders from Washington to serve on a committee to examine quartermasters, and was employed in this duty for three months or more. After a session at Knoxville, Tennessee, Lee having surrendered, we took passage on a steamboat for Chattanooga in high spirits, hoping that the war would soon end and we would be on our way home. As we approached Chattanooga we heard minute guns, and saw the flags at halfmast, and, before the boat had landed, the murder of President Lincoln was announced to us. Our pleasant anticipations of the future were clouded with a darkness that could be felt. A silent grim hatred of Jeff Davis and the other leaders of the rebellion had possession of the Union soldiers then, and if they had been captured no mercy would have been shown.

The surrender of Johnston's army soon followed, and I was ordered to join my corps at Washington. I found the Twentieth Corps encamped in a low damp place northeast, and under command of one of Sherman's favorites, whom he had recently placed in command of the Corps, which retired General Alpheus R. Williams to the command of his division. Williams, who had succeeded Slocum, was a very great favorite with officers and men, and had ably commanded the Corps from Atlanta to North Carolina. I moved camp to a more eligible place — to Corcoran's Hills, a healthy, pleasant camp, which we occupied until the great parade.

The great parade has been described by General Sherman in his memoirs, and by others, and requires no notice from me other than the mention of an incident personal to myself. I was mounted on a beautiful Kentucky-bred mare that felt the occasion, and as we officers of the Twentieth Corps passed the reviewing stand on which were General Sherman and his wife, with the President, and other officers of the government, we saluted, and General Sherman excitedly pointed me out to his wife, exclaiming: "Ellen, there is Duc — Bill Duc, our school fellow at Howe's Academy — there, on that fine horse!" I returned their bow, and the notice was agreeable to me who had not seen Mrs. Sherman since we were children in Lancaster, Ohio.

Senator Fowler of Tennessee, who was acquainted with my work in the Hood campaign on Thomas' staff, took charge of my promotion, and saw it through the senate, and I handed in my resignation, and drew what little pay was due me, and with my wife and three children, went to New York, and to Fire Island next day for a little rest. We went also to Niagara, remaining there a day or two, and then to Mt. Vernon, Ohio, and gathered our possessions together, and shipped them home, — among them a few Angora goats that I had become possessed of during my service on the staff of General Thomas.

How I became interested in Cashmere or Angora goats may as well be told here.

In the vicinity of Nashville was the Belle Meade plantation, owned by Wm. G. Harding, famous as the greatest stock farm in the United States at that time. Beside thoroughbred horses and cattle, and other domesticated animals, Harding had herds of buffalo, elk, deer, and a herd of three hundred Angora goats, ranging in extensive woodland pastures, a constant temptation to the lawless persons who are found in every army. The fine horses — some of them worth thousands each — were especially coveted. Designing persons hatched complaints against Harding for the Provost Marshall, who was induced to send a letter to him which Harding brought to headquarters to lay before General Thomas. Thomas, and all of the staff except myself, were absent, and he asked me to read the notice. This I did, and felt outraged at such a proceeding on the part of the Provost. After some conversation I drew up a reply for him, as follows:

"Colonel Parkhurst, Provost Marshall.

"Sir: I am required by your note to show cause in writing, under oath, why I should not be sent to the enemies' lines, where my sympathies are, and where my friends reside. I would respectfully submit that in justice, public policy, and humanity, each and all, will be found ample reason why I and my family, peaceful, orderly, loyal citizens of the United States should not be banished from all we hold dear on earth.

"Justice, as well as protection is the guarantee of the government to all of it's citizens, and if I have offended either civil or military laws or orders, does not the government grant me a lawful hearing and trial in either a civil or military court beore allowing judgment to be pronounced, and a decree of banishment enforced — a punishment next to the extreme penalty of death?

"I claim to be a loyal citizen of the United States and of the state of Tennessee, and that such I have been from the time when General Buell, with the Army of the United States, advanced and took possession of Nashville and the country around that city. . . .

"When the oath was required by the government I was among the first to take and subscribe to it. It became a part of my duty as a citizen, and the duty was discharged cheerfully and without hesitation, as has been every other requirement of the government from that day to this. I claim, therefore, that the penalty of banishment as seemingly contemplated in the notice would be a proceeding clearly at variance with those principles of justice which should be the foundation of all governments. . . .

"Public policy, I also claim — if the power of banishment be within the scope of provost authority — forbids the exercise thereof against myself, a loyal citizen engaged in the useful and honorable pursuit of farming, at a time when the country is so torn up and disturbed that the state can ill afford to lose either the products or example of the farmer who remains quietly at home in the steady and peaceful pursuit of his vocation; at this time, too, when the rebel army is driven from the state, and when it is thought proper to invite soldiers who, only a few days since were in open rebellion with arms in their hands, to return to their homes and remain peacefully on their farms. I say the enforcement now of the order of banishment seemingly contemplated by your notice seems peculiarly against public policy, and in direct variance with the wise and merciful orders of General Thomas, which I trust will do much to restore quiet to this distracted state. . . .

"Am I asked reasons why I should not be driven . . . from the comforts of a home in which I was born, and in which I and my fathers before me have lived . . . to become, with wife and children, beggars and wanderers among strangers?

"That I have friends and acquaintances in the rebel army is true, but no near blood relations. I have friends and acquaintances also in the union army. Who is there in this internecine war who has not? . . .

"The authorized acts of the government through its proper agents I may not always approve, but that does not alter my duty as a loyal citizen to obey them. That duty has, I claim, thus far been faithfully discharged, whatever tales ignorant gossip, slander, or uncertain spies may have whispered . . . without knowing what charges, if any, are alleged against me, I am at a loss what further, if anything, to offer as an answer to your inquiry. I enclose at a venture this affidavit for your consideration. Sworn to before a proper officer, and signed, W. G. Harding."

This was sent to the Provost Marshall, and nothing more was heard of proceedings against General Harding. (He was general of some militia organization I believe; at any rate he was known to me as General Harding.)

He offered to pay me for my services as his attorney, but I declined. He invited me to go out to his place to see his stock. This I did, and was delighted with the place, and its people and animals, especially pleased with the Angora goats, and I did not refuse the gift of a pair of them, which, with others I bought of another person, I sent to Mt. Vernon, Ohio, to be fed until I could arrange for their transfer to Minnesota. This was accomplished at the close of the war, and I soon had a flock of sixteen beautiful, white, long silky-haired goats, who refused to be satisfied with the grass of my pasture, and loved to destroy all the young trees and bushes in my own yard, as well as the yards of neighbors. They were a beautiful nuisance.

One day an admiring farmer, Mr. Grovenor, who had a place on Trout Brook, (fourteen miles south) on which was much brush, begged the priviledge of taking the flock for three years, on condition of returning the original number, and half the increase, and carried them off to his farm, where they made short work of the brush patches, and were willing to explore neighboring premises, and at the end of two years he was anxious to return both the flock and all the increase. I declined to receive them, and Grovenor turned them over to a Swede, who, I suppose, ate them. Thus terminated my experiment of trying to introduce a valuable breed of goats into Minnesota.

XVIII

A Western Trip

In November 1870 I went to Salt Lake City, and took a friend with me — Robinson. It was late one Saturday evening when we arrived and took rooms at the Townsend House. The proprietor had two wives. His first wife was said to be half crazed by reason of the order of the church that Townsend take another. She lived a very retired life somewhere in the city. The second wife was an English woman who had charge of the hotel, and who was a very efficient manager and a determined person. When Townsend was ordered to take a third wife the black eyed Englishwoman would have none of her about the hotel, but made Townsend house her elsewhere. As landlady Mrs. Townsend number two conducted the hotel in English fashion, seating herself at the head of the table, and serving the food, which was of the best, and admirably prepared. Very early Sunday morning I started out for a walk before breakfast, thinking to go to the fort, to make inquiry for some of my army acquaintances who were yet in the service. As I passed along the street at a rapid pace I joined a pedestrian going my way who greeted me pleasantly with: "Good morning, sir. You are out early."

"Yes, I thought I would take a little walk before breakfast and go over to the fort to call on some old comrades."

"That is rather a long walk. Do you know how far it is to the fort?"

"No, but it is in sight there, not far away."

"You are evidently a stranger to the deception of vision in these mountain altitudes. It is several miles to the fort that looks so near. Look at the mountain in the south. That is where the Little Emma mine is. How far do you think it is from where we stand?"

"About five miles I think."

"Well, that is twenty miles distant. You had better join me if you want before-breakfast exercise. I am superintendant of schools for the city, and am going to arrange for the Sunday School."

I went with him, and was interested in his talk about schools and methods of teaching. When we parted he said: "Brother Brigham is going to preach today, and if you would like to hear him meet me at this corner, and I will give you a good seat."

At the appointed time I met him, and he took me to the church and gave me a seat to the left, in front and on a level with the raised seats of the twelve apostles. Brigham Young occupied the center of the line, and standing there preached — if such a harangue may be called preaching. It was the same kind of verbal slosh I had heard in early days on the frontiers of Ohio, among the ignorant who imagined they had a call to talk to people on religious subjects. Their preaching often took a wide latitude, as did that of "Brother Brigham." The twelve apostles were a study for the physiognomist, and their several stolid faces attracted my attention far more than did "Brother Brigham's" homily. There was not, among them all, a face indicating any goodness or wisdom, but they seemed appropriate tools for the use of a masterful mind such as their leader's. After the meeting the superintendant joined me, and asked how I liked the sermon, and other questions which I answered as truthfully as a desire to avoid giving offense would admit. He seemed not in the least enthusiastic himself over the sermon. He said: "Brother Brigham has plain talk for plain people. You gentiles can't have any idea how harmoniously our system of polygamy works. I would like to have you go home with me and see my family."

I desired information, and said I would go with him with pleasure. I was taken to a one-story brick house standing in a city lot about twenty-five feet from the street fence, at the end of the road. It was a long building, and with three doors on the side, indicating three wives in three separate apartments. He took me into the first door, which opened into a square room, in which was a woman with an infant a few days old. I was introduced to the mother — "This is my wife Susan." Another woman coming in with something for the sick woman was introduced as "My wife

Kate." Five or six children had straggled into the room, and were mentioned as: "My son Tom, by my wife Kate" and "My daughter Julia, by my wife Susan," and so on, until it became decidedly embarrassing, and as soon as possible I escaped, and returned to the Townsend House, having the experience of my first day in Salt Lake City for reflection. Robinson tired of the Mormons and the city, and returned home. I remained, joined a prospector, John Cummings, and worked a prospect hole in American Fork Canyon, the ore of which was of the same kind with that of the Little Emma mine, which had proved such a bonanza. I employed thirty Mormons, and burrowed into the mountain side for three months, taking out and shipping to San Francisco a cargo of good ore, but not finding any great deposit, as in the Little Emma, I closed out and returned home.

The mine in American Fork Canyon was between twenty and thirty miles distant, going by way of the Little Emma, and from there climbing over a spur of the Wausatch Range, which made it necessary to rise to an elevation usually covered with snow, and in places drifted so deep that it was necessary to beat the horses into the drift breast deep, and hang on to their tails, or a rope from the saddle bow, and be pulled through, and then descend down the canyon to a warmer climate. Another way to reach the mine was by way of Provo, a village at the mouth of the Canyon, and then follow up the mountain stream called American Fork, flowing in a narrow gorge, the perpendicular sides of which were more than half a mile in height. By this route the distance was between forty and fifty miles, and was the route I usually traveled on horse back. At the stable where I was in the habit of getting a horse, they gave me on one occasion, a new saddle with leather bound stirrups. These I objected to as being unsafe, as I had on boots with heavy soles that filled the stirrup; but they said it was the only saddle they had, so I was compelled to take it, or go to another stable, and so I consented to use it for that time.

Returning from the mine, after leaving Provo, I had to cross a long, steep hill or shoulder of the range, and as I approached the top I thought I would relieve my tired horse by walking up the remaining very steep part. In dismounting, my right heel struck a rolling stone, and went under the horse, leaving my left foot hanging in the stirrup. The horse was frightened, and jumping sidewise, commenced to drag me down hill. I remember thinking the chances of life for me were but one in three million, and I wished the horse might put his hind foot on my head and crush it, thus rendering me unconscious; and then I thought how distressed my wife and children would be to know my body had been eaten by the coyotes. Then my head bumped against a rock, and I was unconscious for a time. I had tried to get my pistol out and shoot the horse, but pistol and knife belt were gone — dragged off. How my foot got loose from the stirrup is a mystery. I distinctly remember to this day that I thought my wife did it — pushed the stirrup off the boot — but I was some little time unconscious, and when I recovered my senses I saw my horse feeding a little way down the mountain. Feeling myself all over, I found I was not broken, only bruised and strained. I slowly made my way to the horse and mounted, rode on to a Mormon bishop's house, and remained overnight. The next day I rode into the city, and was nursed a few days for my bruises.

XIX

At Brainerd, Minnesota

At the solicitation of Reuben Knapp I purchased a steam mill at Brainerd and employed him to run it. The Northern Pacific R.R. was being built, and crossed the Mississippi River here. The road had been built by contract, and the contractors had made clean profits of about two million dollars. This would have been saved to Cooke if he had adopted the plan I urged upon him at his country place near Philadelphia. I proposed that he let the work be done by enlisted labor. There were many Colonels of regiments who could and would have been glad to enlist a regiment of discharged soldiers, and take a piece of road under the direction of a competent engineer. I proposed that the men be enlisted with the agreement that they might claim and preëmpt a farm from the government lands lying alongside the railroad, and should have the right to drop out of the organization for the purpose of making a farm home. To such would be given certain transportation free for a year or two, the pay of the men to be direct to them by a paymaster, and each one to receive a small bonus in stock of the road, thus making friends for the road, living alongside and furnishing business for the road as soon as it could be built. We discussed the proposition all one afternoon and Cooke said he would sleep on it and in the morning decide. He decided, unfortunately for him, to let the work by contract. He thought the method I proposed would make too much work for him personally, and so the work was done by contract, and cost him three times as much as if it had been done and paid for by day's work.

The sawmill I bought at Brainerd was run for two years with moderate profit, and afterward sold for four thousand dollars. On one of my visits at Brainerd the Reverend Edward Beecher appeared with a fellow traveler — a Mr. Morrell, from Maine. They wanted to go fishing in some of the lakes. As I was always ready to join a fishing party, or make up one, I took them out to Serpent Lake, where there were at that time plenty of black bass and pickerel. Beecher was in my canoe, a birch bark affair, that sat on the water as lightly as an eggshell, with which he had had no experience, and, as we were casting for bass, he had a strike that enthused him, and he turned the canoe from under us. As I came up from the cold bath, and shook the water from my head to swim ashore, I made some comments that were warmer than the water. We set about making a fire by which to dry ourselves. As Morrell came to the shore in his canoe he laughingly called out to Mr. Beecher, "What did you think when you came up out of that cold water?" He said what he thought was not exactly proper for him to say, but it was a good thing to have a friend along to say things for you sometimes. Then I said: "Just for that remark, Mr. Beecher, I am tempted to tell you a story: There was a William Lowry, who came from Pennsylvania, and made a claim and laid it out in the town of Rochester in this state. Bill Lowry was known all along the frontier as a man who was a friend to anyone who had no friends, and he prided himself on such reputation. In starting his town he built a meeting house, which was open for any or every assemblage of people. An enthusiastic missionary came to him and asked the use of the house for the purpose of getting up a revival. Lowry was not a member of any church, and was in the habit of getting full of liquor every Sunday, and sometimes on week days too. "Revival," he said, "revival, yes certainly, Mister, come right along. The boys need reviving, and if you can do it, I'll light up the house for you. It won't cost you a cent."

The meetings were held every night during the week, and on Sunday they were to close. Lowry was at the last meeting, and when the preacher anxiously appealed to the audience: "If there's anybody wants to get religion, let him come to the anxious seat to be prayed for!" Nobody came, and the preacher went on: "If there's any friend of Christ here, let him stand up." No one stood up, until Lowry, steadying himself by the back of a bench, rose and announced: "I'm a friend of Christ — or the friend of any other fellow that hain't got no more friends than *He*'s got in this here crowd!"

147

Mr. Beecher seemed to enjoy the story, and, some three or four years afterward, being in New York City, passing up Broadway, I heard my name called from the opposite side of the street. I saw someone dodging across through the crowded jam of teams, and soon welcomed the Reverend Mr. Beecher, who said, among other pleasant things, that he wanted to thank me for that story of a man who was a friend to anyone who had no friends, for he had used it hundreds of times in his prayer meetings. . . .

An item of knowledge acquired at Brainerd is worthy of record as it may encourage someone to make profitable use of the blueberries that grow wild in such great abundance in Northern Minnesota and elsewhere. A merchant named Bly engaged the Indian women to pick blueberries and shipped them to the St. Paul market; but the berries were so abundant that year that the market was over-supplied, and Bly had a great many left on hand, and more coming every day. A German employed in my mill told me that he was wine maker in Germany, and could make good wine from blueberries. I sent the man to Bly, who engaged him to make the blueberry wine, and, at the end of the season, sent me a keg which I put away in a closet and forgot. Some six or seven years afterward the keg was in the way, and inquiry made as to its contents. I had forgotten all about it until it was opened and found to be a most delicious port wine by some people who claimed to know the different kinds of wine. I knew nothing about port, but I did know it was a keg of Bly's blueberry wine made in Brainerd.

XX

Commissioner of Agriculture

In the year 1877 being offered the position of Commissioner of Agriculture, I accepted it, closed our house at Hastings, rented one in Washington, and assumed the duties of my office on July 1st. Four years of very active work followed, with inadequate compensation, for my salary did not pay my living expenses. When I took charge of the Department it was in contempt of the agriculturists of the country. The organization of grangers was then universal, and they felt and said that the Department was a disgrace to the interest which it was established to represent in the general government as then conducted, and they proposed to have it abolished. It appeared to be chiefly useful for political purposes by members of congress.

When I had held the office some months, the members of the National Grange had a meeting at Richmond, Virginia, and I sent a messenger to them asking them to visit the Department. After the adjournment a large delegation came to see me, and I explained to them my conception of what the Department ought to try to do for the benefit of the farming interest, and invited their cooperation if they approved of my program, and asked them to favor me with suggestions. They heartily endorsed me, and were my staunch friends throughout my entire administration, and were earnestly anxious to have me continued through the next. The effort I made to have the Department advanced to a full equality with other Departments was subsequently realized, and its importance demonstrated on the foundations I had established with the meager means allowed me by Congress during the first year of my administration. At the last Congress gave me all the money I thought proper to ask for. During my four years' term I published for distribution 1,411,625 bound volumes, total pages 801,-626,325; specials and miscellaneous circulars 956.900. Total pages to circulate among farmers and others interested in agricultural matters, 858, 381, 675. These are matters of record, and attest the industry of the limited number of employees in the Department of Agriculture during my term of office.

A few incidents not to be found in the publications of the Department may be found interesting. At the beginning, I read carefully all papers brought to me for signature. A letter to an inquiring farmer covering two sides of a sheet I declined to sign, as there seemed to be only a fog of words saying nothing definite. I sent for the clerk, and for the letter he was expected to answer. Having looked over the letter I asked: "Why did you use so many words, and then not answer the letter?"

"We have been instructed," he replied, "not to commit the Department."

"Not to commit the Department? What are we here for then? Is it not that you know nothing of the matters inquired into? Were you brought up on a farm?"

"No, sir, I was a newsboy in Philadelphia, and worked up to a position as a reporter, and was sent to Washington to report for the paper; and I keep the Department right with such and such papers in Pennsylvania."

"Then I suppose you were billeted on this Department by some member of Congress as correspondent of those papers to help his election?"

"Yes sir, of course."

"Well, I must have as my assistants clerks who know something of these matters. This Department is expected to advance. I cannot have clerks who are here doing the work of congressmen and newspapers. At the end of the month your services will be no longer required."

I ordered the chief clerk to find out if there were other clerks billeted on us by congressmen. He found in all six, whom I ordered dismissed at the end of the month. They were, of course, indignant, and told the chief clerk to tell the Commissioner "that if he turns us out we will open on him all along the line." I asked the chief clerk the meaning of the threat. He said: "There is a combination of all correspondents in this city, and if one is turned out of place, they all resent it, and make life as unpleasant as possible for the government officer. They will ridicule, misrepresent and annoy you whenever they can."

I found this to be true. The newspapers were filled with abuse and ridicule, especially with regard to my efforts to make our own sugar and tea. One day a Scot appeared in my office asking an interview. He said: "On landing in New York City the other day I noticed the papers filled with ridicule of your attempt to grow tea in this country, and I felt that as I passed through Washington, on my way to India, where I have been engaged in the cultivation of tea for sixteen years, I must tell you that undoubtedly you can grow tea in the southern states as well as anywhere, and profitably."

I thanked Mr. Jackson for his call, and information, and finally persuaded him to remain a while and assist me in selecting a proper place for the government tea garden. I directed him to go through the states of North Carolina, South Carolina, and Georgia, and in some place likely to be visited by persons of wealth to select land suitable for our purpose; also to examine and report on some tea plants in those states which were known to us to have been introduced by private individuals for ornamental purposes, or for curiosity. He reported a selection made near Charleston, South Carolina, at a place called Summerville, an old plantation on which the manor house had been destroyed by fire, and the place had grown up to brush and trees, and was the property of Henry A. Middleton, who lived in Charleston. I went down, examined and approved of his selection, and called on Mr. Middleton to bargain for a piece of the old abandoned estate. My card reading 'General Wm. G. Le Duc,' was not a fortunate introduction, for Mr. Middleton was an unconverted rebel, and my reception was decidedly frigid. When I said my visit was for the purpose of buying for the United States Government a portion of the old plantation at Summerville for an experimental tea garden, he said, with some asperity: "I think I have no land to sell to the United States Government. I am buying land."

"Then I regret to have troubled you, sir," I said. "I am the Commissioner of Agriculture for the United States; not for the state of Minnesota, where I live. Agriculture there is in a flourishing condition, and requires no assistance. But the South, ruined by the war, is relying on one crop, cotton, and getting poorer. I

thought to improve the situation by the introduction of tea culture, and wished to turn the twelve million dollars we are now annually sending abroad to other farmers into the hands of the
southern farmers, and I sent a Scot, who had been for some years
familiar with the cultivation of tea in India, through the southern
states to pick out a place where the plant would flourish and be
accessible to observers. When he reported that he had found a
suitable place near Charleston, and that the land was part of an
abandoned plantation belonging to one Middleton, I came down
to make personal examination and approval of his selection; and
when I remembered that a Middleton had signed the Declaration
of Independence, and a Middleton had been governor of South
Carolina, I felt sure I would be able to get the land needed for my
purpose. I find myself disappointed, and I wish you good day, sir."

"Hold a moment, sir," said the old gentleman, (he was eighty-
four then), "that is another view of the matter. I have no land to
sell, but for this purpose I might lease some land. How long a time
should such an experiment be continued by the government?"

"I think twenty years would be necessary and sufficient."

"And how many acres would be requisite?"

"One to two hundred acres ought to be used for the nursery to
propagate plants for distribution, and for production."

"Very well, sir, I have no land for sale, but for this purpose I
will lease to the government the two hundred acres you wish, for
twenty years. Draw up a proper lease and bring it to me, and I
will sign it."

"What consideration, Mr. Middleton, shall I write in the lease?"

"One dollar, sir."

"I will have the lease drawn up and bring it to you tomorrow,"
I said. "I am happy to know that the old patriotic family of Mid-
dletons is not extinct, and wish it may long continue to illustrate
the virtues of its forebears," and I thanked him, and wished him
good day.

I took the lease to him, and when it was signed, paid him a silver dollar. When I returned to Washington I sent to the mint in
Philadelphia and had a silver medal struck, the head of Washington appearing in profile on one side, and on the reverse was the
legend "Paid to Henry A. Middleton, Charleston, South Carolina,
Dec. 29, 1880, by Wm. G. Le Duc, Commissioner of Agriculture of
the U. S. in consideration of twenty years lease of U. S. Experi-

mental Tea Farm." This I had placed in a proper leather covered case and forwarded to Mr. Middleton. I had two duplicates made, one of which I gave to President Hayes, and the other I kept, and have now, this A.D. 1909.

I put Jackson in charge of the place to prepare for a nursery in which to plant the seed I had ordered from India, China, and Japan. Jackson employed a number of laborers, and had to have money to pay bills, and was twenty two miles from a bank or any suitable place to deposit money. There was an old fashioned safe in the basement of the Department which had been discarded for a better and larger one. This I had cleaned and painted and shipped to Summerville for Jackson's use in caring for the books and money of the Department. It was larger than necessary, but cost only the refitting and freight. Newspaper scribblers got hold of the matter, and filled their columns with denunciation of the extravagance of the Commissioner who was throwing away money on the foolish hobby of tea-raising. Now it is only necessary to say that tea cultivation is an established industry, and that no cleaner or better tea is made than at the old plantation at Summerville, the credit for which is mainly due to the persistent effort of Dr. Charles U. Shepard, a Connecticut man of scientific knowledge.

In South Carolina the tea seed was planted on the ground prepared for the nursery. I directed Jackson to go also to Georgia and visit a plantation where Dr. Fortune many years before had planted tea seed, and trees were growing wild, also to go to Georgetown, where a lady I heard of had a few trees, and to gather the leaves of all and make samples of tea. This he did, and sent me the samples. I took three and went to New York City. At the Cooper Institute I met Mr. Peter Cooper, and asked him to recommend to me some honest tea merchant on whose word I could rely for an opinion as to the quality of the tea made from the leaves grown in the United States. Mr. Cooper was much interested in my experiments, and took me down to the office of his old friend Mr. A. A. Low. To him I explained my errand, which was to ascertain if the leaves of the tea plant grown in the southern states would make as good tea as those grown in China or India. "That," he said, "is easily determined. I will send them in to my taster, and he will soon tell us."

This he was about to do when I suggested that he send them in with other teas, without indicating where they were grown. This he willingly assented to, and taking an old Mexican sixpence from his pocket he put it in one cup, with a pair of balances, and thus weighed out a portion from each sample, marked the cups, and, with several other samples, we three went into the tea taster's room, and submitted them for examination. The taster sat at a round table which revolved, and had one or two shelves. At his side he placed a kettle of water over a flame to heat. When it came to the boiling point he turned the water onto the tea in the several cups, and taking out his watch timed the drawing, and then commenced tasting the liquids. The old white-haired gentlemen were sitting behind him, and I was on one side, anxiously watching every motion. As he tasted each cup he would mark it, and say "You can afford to pay thirty cents" — or more, or less — "for the sample in this cup." Soon he came to one of my samples, and said: "Tea of this kind you had better not buy."

"That," I said, "is one of my samples. Will you tell me the reason you reject it?"

"It has not been fired long enough to suit our market."

"Could it not be fired more?" I inquired, not knowing what the firing process was.

"Oh, yes, I suppose so. The leaf seems to be all right."

He proceeded with his tasting, and came to another of my samples. "This," he said, "you can afford to pay forty cents for."

I straightened up. After careful consideration of another of my samples he said: "Fifty cents." I was happy; the highest price he had suggested for any other sample was thirty-five cents, so I put some face on, and said: "I am disappointed that you do not offer me a higher price for these two."

"They would be worth more in London, but not here."

"How much more?"

"Ten cents on each grade."

"Ten cents a pound for carrying them across the Atlantic ocean? That is pretty high freight."

"Yes, but they mix in London, and use these high grade India teas to bring up their low grades."

"But these are not India teas."

"Oh, yes, they are. If you have bought them for something else you are deceived: they were made in the province of Assam."

"No," I said, very earnestly, "I personally know they were not made in Assam —"

He looked at me incredulously, and tasting again said: "Possibly in the neighboring province of Darjeeling."

"No," I said, "neither Assam nor Darjeeling, nor in India at all."

"Maybe," he said, with some slight degree of scorn (for he was paid ten thousand dollars a year to know all about teas), "you think they were made in China or Japan or Ceylon?"

"No."

"Well, I have mentioned all the tea growing countries in the world."

"There is one other," I said, rising in my excitement, "the United States of America — in the state of South Carolina."

The old gentlemen were on their feet too, amused by my excitement, and hurrahed for the United States of America. I said to the taster: "Allow me to say to you that these teas were made by a man who has been engaged in making teas in India for seventeen years, and doubtless made these as he made the India teas, but these are from leaves grown in South Carolina and Georgia, and I have submitted them to the crucial test of price, and find that the American leaf will make as good tea as the best. I desire to thank you for the assurance."

"I think," said Mr. Low, "that although you may grow as good tea leaves in America you will not so easily do away with us old tea merchants. You can't compete with Asiatic cheap labor."

"I certainly do not desire to do away with the old tea merchants, if it were possible, which it is not. There will be merchants as long as there is tea to sell; but when the tea is near home the merchant will not have to wait so long for his profits. As to cheap labor in India — at six cents a day — Mr. Jackson tells me that a negro woman cotton picker at fifty cents a day is cheaper and better than coolie labor at six cents. He says with negro cotton pickers to pick the leaves, he can make such tea as is shown in the samples for eighteen to twenty-two cents a pound, and that most of the work can be done by machinery, the only hand labor being the picking. If Jackson is right, the profit between the cost and the price you offer — forty and fifty cents — is large enough to attract producers and merchants. The questions of cost of production and labor will adjust themselves. What I am trying to do is to demonstrate that a new industry is possible to the farmer of the south, whose only crop now is cotton."

Mr. Low proposed to call a meeting of some of the prominent tea merchants, and have an exhibit of these samples. This was done. I remember the names of Beebee and Anderson only, of those present. My successor in the office of Commissioner of Agriculture disapproved of the experiment of tea culture, and the nursery was permitted to grow up to weeds and run wild for some years. Dr. Shephard, a man of learning and of fortune, who had come south from Connecticut on business as a chemist, noting the condition of the government nursery became interested in matter of tea growing, and devoted himself and his fortune to the business. His example has been followed by others, and the cultivation of tea in the United States is now an assured industry.

In 1904 Dr. Shephard wrote me his crop that year was twelve thousand pounds, and he was extending his gardens annually. His tea is retailed in the large cities for one dollar a pound. I have read in the newspapers that other capitalists have engaged in the industry, notably a company with a paid up capital of fifty thousand dollars. Every farmer in the cotton belt might have a small tea garden, the picking from which would be sent to a central factory for manipulation. . . .

During my administration of the Department of Agriculture the great amount of wheat shipped from the United States alarmed the English farmers, and Parliament sent a delegation of three members to make inquiry into the condition of our agriculture, and the probability of a continuance of such large exports of wheat. Mr. Read, M. P., and another were introduced to me by Sir Edward Thornton, the British minister, at the Department, and at his request I made out a route for them to embrace the wheat growing sections of our country, up through the northwest, and then down through Iowa, Kansas, Missouri, Arkansas, Texas, and back to Washington through the southern states, giving them letters of introduction to various railroad magnates, who would, I knew, be quite ready to show off their roads and adjacent lands. They said they had the most astonishing ride of their lives, and no longer wondered where the immense crops of wheat came from.

The Paris exposition occurring during my term of office, I sent a young doctor of philosophy, William McMurtrie, to represent the Department, and get all the information possible of the manufacture of sugar from beets, and the manufacture of wine and brandy from grapes. His work was very satisfactory, interesting and useful, and is of record. On his return I set him to examine the wools of an exhibit of sheep, the report of which was of scientific value, though not of interest to people generally. In making an examination of wool from individual animals of different breeds he had arranged a table with devices for the microscopic examination of each fibre of wool with reference to the length, strength, and number of imbrecations to the inch. An old sheep farmer whom I had met at the sheep show, and had urged to come down from the mountains of Pennsylvania and visit the capital of his country, came, and I took him to the room where Dr. McMurtrie was engaged in the examination of wool. He happened to have in the machine a fibre of wool from the old farmer's best ram, and said to him: "Your ram seems to have been sick for about ten days or two weeks last April."

"Sick?" said the farmer. "No, that ram has not been sick."

"Do you keep a record of the condition of your fancy stock?"

"Of course I do."

"Won't you look when you go home, and see if anything was the matter with that ram the first two weeks in April?"

"I can do that now; I have the book in my pocket," and he referred to his book, and found, to his astonishment, that the ram was off his feed at the time indicated, and was much mystified until the Doctor showed him through the microscope that portion of the fibre that must have grown during that period. It was flatter and thinner than other portions of the fibre. The old farmer was amazed to know that a man sitting in an office in a distant city could tell him the condition of his animal at a certain time, and this he considered the most astonishing thing he had seen in Washington.

In the year 1877 some friends in St. Paul wrote asking me to persuade the President to visit the State Agricultural Fair that autumn. George Finch, a merchant, was at the head of the enterprise, and General Sibley and others were exerting themselves to make it a notable occasion. I joined in the scheme, and escorted the President and Mrs. Hayes, with other guests from Washington, to the fair at St. Paul, and to see some of the great wheat fields of Dakota from which were coming the immense quantities of wheat which made possible the great milling properties at Minneapolis. After the visit to the fair and to the Dakota farms the Presidential party paid a visit to Hastings. Our house had been closed in our absence, but our neighbors offered their services, and the necessary preparations were made properly to receive the party and give them a luncheon, and have a public reception at the courthouse before we took the cars for Washington.

The St. Paul fair was a great success, and laid the foundation for the great annual fair now held there. The versatile William King tried to change the location by having a Minneapolis fair in 1878. This fair I attended, and was being taken through the very fine display of agricultural productions and livestock, when, passing up a stairway, I saw, sitting by itself, without label or notice of any class to which it might belong, a common horse bucket filled with brown sugar, and standing beside it a flat patent medicine bottle filled with a bright clear syrup. I said "What does this mean, Mr. King?" He replied, "I do not know," and called someone who had that part of the show in charge, who informed us that it was a bucket of sorghum sugar that old Seth Kenney had brought and set down there with a bottle of syrup; that he was in the habit of making such an exhibit of sugar and syrup at every fair. I was intensely interested and found the sugar first class brown, granulated sugar, and the syrup clear and thick as strained honey.

"Come on," said King, "I want to show you my fine imported bulls."

"Excuse me Mr. King," I said, "this bucket of sugar is of more importance than all the bulls in America and Europe. We are importing between one and two million dollars worth of sugar annually, raised by farmers of other countries, and shipped into a country where a farmer with crude implements in Minnesota makes it of sorghum. Where is Mr. Kenney?" Kenney could not be found, and it was ascertained that he had gone home. In reply to a letter requesting him to return he said he was busy with his sorghum, and could not leave home. I sent a man to learn and report the variety of sorghum he used, and his manner of cultivation and treatment in making sugar and syrup, and to obtain samples. The problem of the supply of one of the great necessities of our mode of life from the fields of our own farmers seemed possible.

The cultivation of cane in Louisiana and other gulf states furnished but a small part of the large amount necessary, and climatic conditions forbade the extended cultivation of tropical cane. But in Europe beets had been demonstrated to contain a profitable amount of sugar, and the juice of the corn plant was, as every farmer's boy who had hoed corn knew, full of saccharine matter; and the report of Lane to Sir Walter Raleigh, A.D. 1585, in which he describes the new found corn plant, and the uses made of it by the Indians, says: "The cane makes good and very perfect sugar." With these sources of sugar why should the United States continue to import it from foreign countries?

On my return to Washington I submitted a sample of the sugar made by Kenney to Doctor Collier, the chemist at the Department, for critical examination, and it was found to be the equivalent of the best cane sugar. Also, an appreciable amount of cane sugar was found in the stalks of common corn. To popularize the making of sugar a complete apparatus was purchased and installed in the Department grounds and put in the hands of Doctor Collier. A piece of land was rented and planted to Kenney's early amber cane, and other varieties of sorghum which were favorites in other states, but which had not been thoroughly examined with reference to making granulated sugar. Hedges in Missouri, and Schwartz in Illinois were active in experiments with varieties of sorghum, and I sent Doctor Richardson to procure new varieties of tropical cane for the promotion of the sugar industry in Louisiana, and in other ways endeavored to encourage the sugar planters of the gulf states whose mills were standing idle since the war. An association of sugar planters was organized, and the new varieties of tropical cane secured by Doctor Richardson were turned over to them. They were encouraged to try to make sugar with paid labor instead of slave labor, which they had declared to be impossible. A delegation of this organization called on me at the Department to express gratification because of the interest I had manifested in their business. The delegation consisted of the president, Duncan Kenner, John Diamond, and several others whose names I do not now recall. After some pleasant conversation I handed them a jar of sugar, and asked them to examine it and express an opinion as to it's quality. The jar was passed around, receiving favorable comment, and some one asked where it was made. I said: "Cannot you experts tell?" Some guessed one place, and some another, but all were confident it was made in one of the gulf states, and was open pan work. When I assured them it was made by a Minnesota farmer, from sorghum, they looked at each other in silence, as if the end had come, and they were defeated. One of them said, dejectedly, "It is no use for us to spend thousands of dollars in new machinery, for some infernal Yankee will come along and start up a new thing that will ruin us."

"But," I said, "let us see if there is not a hopeful side to it. The profit in your machinery is in running it. With the tropical cane you can run only thirty or forty days in the year. There are many varieties of sorghum. The early amber ripens in ninety days, the other varieties in four or five months. Our chemist assures us that there is as much sucrose in many varieties of sorghum as there is in the tropical cane you are using; and that there is a paying quantity in corn stalks at the present price of sugar. Why not plant sorghum to keep your mills running half the year?" Kenner said: "Well, you have given us something to think about. Certainly our country ought not to import sugar, if it can be made at home, as seems probable."

When I turned over the Department to Doctor Loring the country was much interested in the production of home sugar, and the able chemist of the Department, Doctor Collier, was enthusiastic in the belief and advocacy of making it from sorghum and corn stalks and beets. I had appropriations from Congress in aid of beet sugar factories, and had imported machinery for them from Germany, but the results were not satisfactory chiefly because we had not at that time the labor in the country that was familiar with the culture of the beet, and our native farm labor accustomed to cultivate growing crops riding on a double sulky cultivator, would not get down on hands and knees and weed beets, as was necessary and customary in European states. But with sorghum the manner of cultivation was familiar and agreeable, and it was grown in every state in the union. The problem remaining to be solved was to determine the process by which sugar could be certainly granulated from the syrup without fail. This was the problem which the chemist was intent upon, and when Loring disapproved of sorghum and all that belonged to it, Doctor Collier resigned. The day is yet to come when we will cease to import sugar from Europe or from tropical countries, but come it must, when the large amount of sugar consumed in the United States is made at home where it should be.

Hog cholera and pleuro-pneumonia and Texas fever were prevalent and increasing, and affecting our trade at home and abroad. I established a bureau of animal industry and employed competent veterinary surgeons to inspect herds, and control the spread of disease as far as possible. A charge of pleuro-pneumonia made in England against cattle shipped from the United States caused serious loss to shippers, and interruption to trade, and this charge being made repeatedly against cattle shipped from our ports with a clean bill of health convinced me that there was something wrong on the other side. I sought and found a well educated veterinary surgeon, a Harvard man, and sent him with an assistant to inspect the work of the English people. The result was that they were compelled to acknowledge their wrong, and our cattle shipments went on as before. It was, apparently, a scheme to put up the price of English cattle. The young veterinarian who fought the Britons on their own ground was Doctor Charles P. Lyman, who felt much gratified with his success — as did I. Twenty-eight years after I was fishing for rock cod from the dock of the beautiful Tacoma park that fronts on Puget Sound, when a man who was evidently an invalid approached and entered into conversation about fishing. Some friend came along who, recognizing me, called me by name. The invalid was startled, and looking at me exclaimed: "Can it be possible that you are General Le Duc, who was Commissioner of Agriculture in Hayes' administration? Do you remember sending someone to England on an important mission?" "Yes, I sent a young fellow fresh from Harvard, one Doctor Lyman, over there, and he had to fight all the English veterinarians they could gather at Liverpool, but by calling in the aid of his old professor from Edinburgh he routed the Englishmen, and secured a right decision."

The invalid straightened himself up, and said: "I am Doctor Lyman."

I looked at him and said: "You are not the Doctor Lyman I sent on that important duty. He was a young man — it can't be possible."

"You must remember, General," he answered, "that that was many years ago. Why, I have been a lecturer in Harvard for nineteen years since that time." He was in Tacoma for his health, and we had many pleasant meetings before my return to Minnesota. He has wandered to various parts of the United States, and finally settled at Whittier, California, and bought a little fruit farm. . . .

XXI

At Work as Commissioner

Some members of congress from New York, prompted by the learned and industrious Doctor Hough, had procured an appropriation of a few thousand dollars to be expended by the Department of Agriculture for a preliminary treatise on forestry, and the work was begun before I assumed direction of the Department. The report was made to me, and I saw so much of importance in it that I had a large edition of it printed, and I organized a division of forestry, and put Doctor Hough at the head of it. From this beginning has grown the earnest attention the government is now giving to the important interest of forestry in the United States. I sought to have the Coteau du Prairie, a height of land on the western border of Minnesota and eastern border of Dakota, extending from Big Stone Lake to the Missouri at Sioux City, reserved from entry, and reforested, as it was at one time densely covered with timber, which retained the rainfall and fed the Jim River and other streams, the channels of which are almost dry. But I failed to convince the members of congress of the importance of this action, and now the land is in the hands of individual owners.

During the winter of 1882 I received notice of my election as a member of the National Agricultural Society of France. The honor of an election to membership of this ancient and famous society was not fully appreciated until I learned that but few Americans before me had been honored in like manner. These were George Washington, Count Rumford, (Benjamin Thompson), Thomas Jefferson, and John Marshall. Since then I learn that one, and possibly two others have been added. One, I am sure, is Doctor Howard, entomologist of the Department of Agriculture.

The administration of President Hayes drawing to a close, the Department officers were requested to send in suggestions as to subjects to be mentioned in his message. I thought it a robbery of the birthright of the children born in the United States to permit foreign nations to send their surplus population, — destitutes, vagrants, and some criminals — to land on our shores, to be given a hundred and sixty acres of land, and invested with the ballot. I recommended a very stringent restriction of immigration, prohibiting all but the best. Knowing this would meet with violent opposition from land speculators and all transportation companies, I took my recommendation to one of the members of the cabinet — an old friend of mine — and read it to him. His remark was: "You are right, Le Duc. Immigration ought to be discouraged and limited; but politically I would not have the courage to say so." I said, "Well, isn't it our duty to say and do the thing we believe to be right, and let the consequences take care of themselves." He answered: "Let us see what the President will say about it." I took it to the President and urged him to put such a recommendation in his message. He finally said: "This question of immigration is a great and difficult question. We are going out of office. I think we had better leave the responsibility for those who follow us."

And it was left, and Europe has dumped upon us her criminals, agitators, and theorists — along with some good people. These have taken up the land that should have been saved for our children, and, strangers to our form of government, are availing themselves of our folly by taking out of our hands the government of the country.

Among other incidents during my term of office in Washington was a familiar acquaintance with the brilliant member of congress from New York City, the Honorable S. S. Cox, whose wife and mine were intimate friends in their Putnam Seminary days. With "Sunset Cox" I had frequent occasions to exchange pleasantries. I desired to eliminate from the Department the distribution of seeds as then in vogue, which I regarded as a graft, insisted upon by members of Congress for their personal benefit; and as Cox was in the opposition I appealed to him to assist me in correcting the abuse. To this he willingly assented in conversation. I received from him this characteristic letter:

"United States Hotel, Saratoga Springs
"Sept. 1879

"My dear General: After acknowledging yours with regard to poultry, and promising you my best coadjutancy in the proper appropriation of money for the best purposes — to wit, that your Department shall do what private enterprise will not or cannot do — I have the honor to enclose you this peculiar epistle with the catalogue. The writer, Mr. Seaver, is the editor of Harpers Drawer, and he is always happy. How he dares to venture to ask, at this season, of a member of congress summering at Saratoga, early Dutch drumheads and top onion sets and such like, is beyond my comprehension. This is not the way to begin our reform. However, if you have anything suitable for culture now, and can send to him, Seaver, you will find his friend Tallboys will grow taller. Yours, S.S. Cox"

Seaver's letter enclosed was as follows:

"Dear Cox: My friend, Tallboys, is deeply exercised on the seed question, and wished very much to get the kind mentioned on the opposite page. I don't happen to know the federal gardener, and therefore venture to ask you to make such an appeal to that functionary as will wring from him the desired what d' you call 'ems.

"Your seedy friend,
"Wm. A. Seaver"

The list was dated Union Club, West 21st Street, and read: "Red beet seed, early Dutch drumhead cabbage, turnip, rutabaga, olive-shaped raddish, drumhead lettuce, top onion sets, cucumber seed, tomato, butter beans. Dear Seaver, this is the list of seed from the Patent Office.

"Yours forever,
"Tallboys"

This was a fair sample of the working of the iniquity at this time. Two friends met at a city clubroom. Tallboys, wanting garden seeds, was not acquainted with a member of congress, and his friend Seaver was, and rather than go to a seed store and buy the desired seed he asked his friend to obtain it for him through a member of congress, who was authorized to demand it, Congress having appropriated between one and two hundred thousand dollars for the purchase of seed to be put up in little papers for members of congress to send to voters in their districts. Although condemned by many yet there has been a majority in favor of this practice.

I had other communications from the witty editor of Harper's Drawer.

"187 Broadway, New York, January 4, 1879

"I am greatly obliged to you for the agricultural report for 1877. Curiously enough, although not coming strictly in the domain of wit, I have in my library fifteen volumes of agricultural reports up to and including 1871. I lack '72 to '76 inclusive. Should you happen to have these volumes and send them to me, I should forever cherish your memory as the chiefest and goodest of all Agricultural Commissioners that have ever existed. For although a cockney in New York devoted to the peaceful and ennobling pursuits of avarice I am fortunate enough to live fourteen miles from town in Westchester County, where I have a few inches of ground. In the city my daily struggle is to raise money enough to enable me in the country to raise the encouraging potato, the cheerful beet, and the consolatory turnip; to drink the lacteal juice of the Alderney, and be whirled behind the tails of nimble Hambletonians. Having enjoyed these, I do my little drawer.

"My great and gallant friend, S. S. Cox, M. C. spends a good portion of his lively existence in talking or writing to me encomiastic adjectives about yourself.

"Very respectfully,
"W. A. Seaver"
House of Representatives, Washington, D.C.
May 1st, 1880

"Dear General: It is sure that you don't give us city people a fair distribution according to our demerits. I take no stock in equity unless it is equal. There is an idea that all agricultural people are denizens of a prairie, or some other ground. My district is full of them. I want a little more recognizance so as to keep peace. Will you send me a lot en bloc? Don't others get them? If got, I will go over my lists and fill the lower end of New York with your glory — morning glory.

"Yours,
"S.S. Cox"

His district was Tammany. I replied:

"Yours requesting a lot en bloc is received. You are late. The custom of the Department is to close the distribution on the fifteenth of April, by which time the *suburban* farmer knows he should have his seed in hand, if not in the ground, but the *urban* farmer of your district cannot be expected to keep as well posted in agricultural stocks as in those of railroads and mines, so, after dusting the seed room, I send you the package.

"'I give thee all I can, no more, though poor the offering be,
This little lot exhausts the store of every seed I see. . . .'
I subscribe myself unofficially but urbanely yours,

"Wm. G. Le Duc"

A naval officer informed me that a native potato found in Peru was so much esteemed by the captains sailing in the Pacific that they would go a hundred miles out of their course to obtain a supply. I sent to our consul at Lima, and had two bushels purchased and shipped to me. They were enclosed in an air-tight wooden box and shipped by the fastest freight, but when the box arrived and was opened the potatoes were rotten. Only a few eyes were secured from the mass and were turned over to Superintendent Saunders to grow if possible, and a few were sent to a friend of the President and of his private secretary, William K. Rogers, who referred to me the letter he received, which was as follows:

"My dear William: Potatoes—Peru potatoes, that is the question. You will observe that I am a farmer by profession and occupation. True it is—and pity 'tis, 'tis true—that I pass some of my leisure moments in playing Judge; but as a steady thing I am an agriculturalist. I fulfill the scriptural cuss; in the perspiration of my forehead I consume my daily rations. Therefore it is that I want Peru potatoes. I see that Le Duc has been there and yanked up a few to the states, and I want my share. Wouldn't bother you, but it is too far to Peru for walking purposes. If the General will send me one, two or three, whatever may be my proportion, I will plant, hoe, grub, and report on the same. If there is anything that springs out of the ground that I am simply tremendous upon it is potatoes. I have now raised my own potatoes nigh on to fifteen years. They are not a cheap food for the masses; mine cost me, last year, a dollar and a half a-piece. Still, as I often say to my wife, though not cheap, they are our own.

"Last year we had bugs—that is, not in the house, but in the potatoes. They came from Colorado—walked all the way, and a very pretty vermin they were. They do not come singly, but in battalions. I said to the boys: 'If you will go to work and fight the bugs, I will give you five cents for every hundred you kill. I have three boys, and they confederated and combined together to the discomfiture of the bugs, and the depletion of my coffers. For two days they worked in the potato patch like beavers. At the end of that time they brought in a bill against me of eighteen dollars and fifty cents. I stood aghast. They showed me the bugs. They measured four bushels and several pecks. I asked if they would take the potatoes for part pay — the whole crop being worth, at ruling rates, about two dollars and seventy cents. They replied that they couldn't see it at all. They further observed that I had been advocating specie payment, and making speeches about the dollars of the daddies, and what they wanted was the dollars of their Daddy. So I had to ante, and you will see, therefore, that I have an affection for the plant, and if the General will send me some I will be obliged."

He was one of the best judges of the Ohio courts, and one of the wittiest of men.

I replied: "Dear Rogers: Some infernal tadpole of the press who has just shed his caudle appendage, and got his frog's mouth on him, by some hocus-pocus known only to the devil, now that the magician, Heller, is defunct, found out that I had obtained two bushels of potatoes from Peru, and forthwith commenced: 'Peru — Peru — Peru —', and then some bigger frogs took it up, 'Peru — Peru — Peru —', until every last frog in the puddle was roaring 'Peru — chuck', as he dived to avoid the missiles hurled at him. It reminds me of the spell of weather described by that Yankee: "First it blew, and then it snew, and then it thew right smart, and then it friz' — as I ought to do, for of course I violate the law when I distribute a potato to a judge, and he ought to know better than to ask it; but regard for his winning ways will carry off a yellow peruvian to him tomorrow."

On the advent of General Garfield as President I tendered my resignation to take effect at the close of the fiscal year, and turned over the Department to my successor, Dr. Loring.